FIFTY ACRES, MORE or LESS

BY

TIMA SMITH

amarok books

Fifty Acres, More or Less

Copyright © 2016 Tima Smith

tima@writingsite.com

Cover Design and Art © 2015 by Lauren Hall & Ted Hall

All rights reserved.

No part of this book may be reproduced in any form or by any electronic or mechanical means (except in the case of brief quotations embodied in articles or reviews) without written permission from its publisher.

amarok books

ISBN: 978-1-944932-22-0

THIS BOOK IS DEDICATED TO

MY PATERNAL GRANDMOTHER

ERNESTA MAGNI GALLERANI

(1871-1952)

WHO DID MUCH HARDER THINGS

PREFACE

A first draft of this book was completed over twenty years ago. I kept putting off refining it because I rarely had the time it was going to require. Friends and family knew about the book and often urged me to finish it. Finally, I've done that.

Somewhat recently, one of my sons suggested that I add a 'back-story' to the book. An answer to the question 'why?' It's a question I've been asked many times. Why did you do it? Why did you undertake this massive project? A project that took years of your life, one that most people would never even consider.

I thought about it for quite a while, not certain I wanted to share such a personal story, but finally decided to go ahead and add it. Not because I consider it particularly fascinating or noteworthy, but because in some way it is intrinsic to the tale of building the house. Building the house was the back-story's antidote, its doppelganger, a physical rebuilding of what had been torn down, lost. And since this is the only memoir I'll ever write, perhaps at some time in the future, it will flesh out the family story.

The back-story appears as very short interim 'chapters' following Book Chapters 6 - 13, with a final interim chapter after Book Chapter 27. Skipping them is always an option.

I've included seven pages of photos following Chapter 5. Although I rarely wanted to stop and search for the camera and film while we were building the house, somehow I managed to take enough pictures to fill an album, Those I've chosen to include are a brief visual guide from the very start of the project until the house was complete.

CHAPTER ONE

It was dawn, it was January, it was freezing.

I lay there listening to the remnants of last night's storm blow out in fitful gusts through the surrounding pines, and when I inched the blanket off my face, the air was so cold it made my skin ache. Sheets of ice crystals covered the insides of the windows and a layer of frost whitened the rough plywood floor. It was the winter of 1986. Not a good winter.

In the woods behind the small unfinished outbuilding we euphemistically called 'the cabin,' I heard deer making their way through the frozen snow. They came every morning just as the air lightened enough to show the outlines of all the things piled around me. I'd first heard them in early October, right after we gave up the tent and got the roof on the cabin. Moving through the leaves, they'd sounded more like a herd of elephants, and I remember getting out of bed and running to the doorway to see what on earth was making such a racket.

Startled, they bounded away through the trees, too many to count accurately ... eight, nine, ten ... including two white-spotted fawns, all their tails showing white, pointed straight at the sky.

In October, they were a symbol of everything that was right with this place ... the untouched nature of it, the chance it offered

Tima Smith

for a less complicated, more self-sufficient life. Starting over, that's what we were doing.

We were still hopeful then.

The days were warm, the sky a brilliant blue, the trees a mass of yellow orange red. We were sure we would finish enough of the house we were building to get into it before winter, and as I watched the deer bolt away that first morning, frightened by my presence in a place where they'd never encountered anyone before, the experience made me ridiculously happy.

But it was January now.

And I wasn't happy. I had absolutely no desire to get up and look at deer. No desire to get up, period. Not to another short, gray, freezing day where we'd only manage to inch along the house that hadn't been ready in September or October, hadn't been ready by Christmas, and certainly wouldn't be ready by February or March or even, probably, April.

So I lay there under five stiff blankets and a sleeping bag, on top of sheets that hadn't been washed in two months because clean sheets had gone the way of everything else that was too inconvenient or too tangential to house-building to be even remotely significant. I'd gone to bed wearing the same two pairs of socks, the same thermal underwear, the same turtleneck and sweat pants and sweatshirt I'd worn the day before, and probably the day before that and the day before that.

At some point in the past, I'd heard about country people donning winter underwear in November and not removing it until April or May, and I'd had a proper response. But wearing the same clothes for days or even months didn't seem disgusting anymore, merely rational.

I lay there looking at the emerging shapes of my plants in the gray dawn. They were the first thing I saw every morning — spiders, dracaenas, figs, ferns, succulents — some of which I'd nurtured ten years or more. Except now they were all dead. They'd died during the first thirty-degree night of the season, and what I needed to do was toss them all out into the snow. A simple thing. A dozen heaves through a doorway with only a tarp and no door.

For one thing we could use the space, and for another we had enough things to remind us of plans gone thoroughly awry without having to look at a bunch of dead plants every morning. But for some reason I hadn't done it. I just didn't have that kind of energy anymore. For throwing out dead plants, changing sheets, going to the Laundromat. I did other things now. We *both* did other things, Art and I. We measured and cut 2x4s, carried sheets of plywood up and down ladders, hauled bricks and cement blocks, hammered nails, drilled holes, pulled wire, searched wrecking yards for building materials, and tried to keep the bright blue water tank from freezing every night. We also tried to keep the bank from finding out that every payment of our construction mortgage was narrowly made.

Every morning I stared at the silhouettes of my plants, their dead branches, their shriveled leaves, and wondered if and when we'd actually be able to complete this thing we'd begun and why for god's sake we'd ever thought it was a good idea in the first place.

My plants were supposed to be thirty yards away in a warm cozy house with a wood stove and lots of windows. Art and I were supposed to be there, too, along with all the stuff piled to the cabin

ceiling around the sofa bed. Furniture. Clothes. Dishes. Books. Boxes full of things we'd already forgotten we even owned.

Lady, our Labrador Retriever, shifted her weight on the rug beside the sleep sofa, and I thought how this was no way for her to be spending her thirteenth winter. I reached down and shifted her blanket until it covered her completely, and she opened one eye, looked up at me and sighed.

The cabin had been the first thing we built, a place to store our things until the house was finished. And moving into it from the

Tima Smith

tent, where we'd spent the summer, should have been a step up. Except once we started on the house, we never finished the cabin. So although it had a roof, walls, a floor, and a few hasty and mismatched windows, the eaves were still wide open, there was no door, no insulation, no electricity. Certainly no toilet, no running water, no heat.

    Back in October, none of these things had mattered. There were birds singing in the morning, the sun was still strong enough to feel warm on your skin, and the noise of deer behind the cabin at dawn was a wondrous thing.

    Funny, the difference a few degrees and a few months could make.

    The tacked-in aluminum-framed window rattled in a gust. The sky was growing lighter. The shapes of all the boxes piled against the 2x4 stud walls began to separate from the shadows. I could see the outline but not the content of an Eakins poster, although by now I didn't have to *see* it to see it. It was a working study of a racing shell on the water, with the artist's reference lines and perspectives, the only thing worth staring at inside the cabin. It was meant to be hanging in the house by now — framed and matted, a reflection of our taste, our style. Instead, it was hanging from a sixteen-penny nail, its corners curled, puckers running its length from the damp cold.

    Hanging it had been a sort of schizophrenic act ... on one hand, an effort to introduce some grace into these primitive surroundings; and on the other, an admission that we were beyond all grace. We'd blundered badly, made bad decisions based on little more than chutzpa and whimsy. And now we were paying for it.

    And we weren't kids. We should have known better.

    Between me and the poster, a Coleman lamp hung from the ceiling looking like a tall man wearing a tall hat. It was the light Art read his students' papers by, the light I'd written a half-dozen stories by. It even gave a bit of heat; which, if we had any sense of

Fifty Acres, More or Less

humor left, might have been funny ... the idea of raising the air temperature immediately around the lamp from, say, twenty-two degrees to thirty-five or even thirty-six.

On top of everything, this was turning out to be the winter to end all winters. Perhaps a special message from the gods, punishing us for our hubris.

Another heavy gust rattled the window and I wondered if the shell of the house had sustained any damage during the night, if the wall-bracing had held, if the third-floor walls were still standing. Because on this hilltop, a forty-mile per hour wind roared through the trees like a freight train. And the storms had come one after the other, through the late fall and into the winter, until it seemed it was the wind's specific intent to keep trying until it blew down at least part of the roofless skeleton sitting in the clearing.

Experience said the shell was stronger than my perception of it, but there was something about the fact that all the studs, all the nails, all the angles holding the house together were self-applied by two people who had come late to those kinds of skills that tended to undermine my confidence. On one hand, everyone who knew something about it told us we'd overbuilt; 2x6s instead of 2x4s; 6x6s instead of 4x4s. Still, I wasn't convinced.

And of course the storms came almost always when Art was off teaching in Boston and I was alone, and that fact was wearing me down. I was sick of weather reports predicting gusts up to sixty. Sick of that spidery feeling I got in the pit of my stomach. Tired of getting solo practice climbing ladders to the third floor so I could step from narrow stringer to narrow stringer with a flashlight under my chin, while I carried another sixteen-foot 2x3 to help brace a new wall.

I hated heights.

Late in the afternoon, Art would be back from two days of teaching in Cambridge. He'd have slept in a clean, comfortable bed, used a toilet that flushed, taken showers with steamy hot water, eaten good hot meals, and mingled with students and

Tima Smith

colleagues who talked about ideas and politics and where they were heading for vacation in February. He was a professor of literature and writing roughing it in the woods like Thoreau, but not enjoying it nearly as much.

Then a shaft of sunlight formed a weak circle on the wall and as if an alarm had gone off, I got out of bed. I couldn't sleep past dawn anymore. Dawn brought light to work by, and there was too much to do to waste any of that light staying warm under the covers — especially when night came crashing down at four o'clock every afternoon.

At least sleeping fully-dressed saved time.

I pulled on my oldest son's oversized blue down jacket, two pairs of gloves, yanked my frozen boots off the floor and laced them on. When I pulled on my snow hat, I got an oily whiff of unwashed hair and had a sudden urge to put Lady in the car and drive the half-hour to the University of Connecticut in Storrs, where I could stand under a hot shower in my oldest daughter's dorm until my skin wrinkled. But the car was in Cambridge and by the time Art came back I'd be too tired to make the trip, and tomorrow we planned to finish the interior stud walls on the second floor front bedrooms, which hardly required clean hair. So for another few days I'd continue to look like any average street person; although there were no mirrors to record it so did it really matter? Besides, vanity had gone the way of grace and clean sheets.

I patted Lady. "You stay here," I told her. She looked grateful.

I walked down the wooden ramp that connected the pole-built cabin to the ground out into a silent frigid world. The branches of a hundred hundred trees were silhouetted against a gray sky, and as I walked down the path the snow squeaked under my boots and a Pileated woodpecker began to shriek, its call receding as it flew away from my disturbing presence. They were easier to spot now among the bare trees, but bird watching was rarely on my agenda anymore, and as I emerged from the woods into the clearing, it was a relief to see that the house was still there, all of it.

Fifty Acres, More or Less

The gigantic blue tarps that were supposed to keep out the rain and snow and did absolutely no good at all flapped and cracked slowly in the wind, and I looked toward the driveway at the tiny white and gray trailer where Lauren lived. She was spending her junior year of high school in a way neither of us ever could have imagined. Her three brothers and sister were in warm dorm rooms from Washington state to Connecticut, but Lauren was stuck here in this mess along with us. The house she'd grown up in was gone, her childhood friends far away, she'd attended three schools in two years. Like Art, she was gone today, staying at a friend's house, getting a break.

With everything else that had gone wrong, it was Lauren's predicament that bothered me most of all. Because a mother wasn't supposed to do things like this to her daughter.

But then I looked at the house, and as it did every morning, my mind let go of everything except all the things there were to do.

A roof to put on, second-hand windows to strip and install, exterior doors to build and hang, siding, stairs, interior framing, and then all the things we couldn't even begin until the weather turned civil — plumbing, wiring, insulation, a chimney, bathrooms, a kitchen.

Looking at the big picture always had the effect of paralyzing me. Where to start? Where to start?

Construction debris lay all around — five months worth of cut stud ends, plywood sheets, slabs of blue rigid insulation frozen in the snow, and, beyond the debris, the surrounding woods. "At least you'll never need a lawn mower," someone had joked. But eventually something was going to have to be done about the trees, too. Because if we intended to make good on our passive solar plan, a lot of them had to come down and be turned into firewood.

That morning, though, clearing half an acre of land so the sun could reach windows that weren't even installed was very far down on our list of priorities.

Tima Smith

I headed for the outhouse.

It was mornings like these, when the trees cracked from the cold and the outhouse seat was a block of ice, when there were 100 2x4s and 70 sheets of 3/4" ply and 25 sixty-pound roof rafters still to raise thirty feet off the ground, when the weather report was for another snowstorm over the weekend that would fill the second floor with yet another foot of snow, ice, eventually water ... it was mornings like these that made me wonder why building a house had ever seemed like a wonderful, exciting solution ... for a minute ... for a second ... for any time at all.

CHAPTER TWO

Call it naiveté or foolish optimism. Call it impulsiveness, impetuousness, over-confidence, stupidity. Certainly it was a case of overreach. Possibly a form of mild dementia.

Though at the time it *did* seem like a good idea.

Let's build a *house*. No, it was more like, let's *build* a house. Because Art and I had been looking for over a year for a place to buy, preferably a fixer-upper since that was all we could afford. And we wanted some land, a couple of acres if possible. Privacy.

I, for one, wanted nothing to look at outside the windows in any direction except trees and sky. We were writers, readers. We didn't want noise, distraction, smoke drifting in from the neighbor's bar-b-cue. We both needed healing. Art, from an overactive thyroid that had made him sick for a year before it was correctly diagnosed. Me, from a seventeen-year-long marriage that had taken its toll in more ways than I knew and from a divorce that had gone inter-planetary in its absurdity.

More than anything, I wanted a home for my kids. Five teenagers whose lives had come apart just when they most needed a strong core to float away from and bounce back to. But we'd gone and deconstructed the home they'd grown up in, my ex-husband and I, and it was almost a frenzy in me to give them a new one. A better one, I hoped. Though eventually I learned that replacement isn't possible, and even if it were, the way we were going about it was taking far too long. Children don't stay children, don't wait around while you try to fix your mistakes.

But back when the decision to buy land and build was made, I was in a place where there was nowhere to go but up. At least that's what I thought. I was starting over again. New partner. New state. New home. New me. Well ... as new a me as me could get. And with all this to do, with all this to deal with ... five teenagers

Tima Smith

whose lives had been fractured, no reliable prospects for income, no help, nothing to fall back on, and with Art terribly weakened from his malady ... with all this we decided to *build a house!*

A house. A kind of heavy-handed symbol you might say, and you might say right. Because the house and the life have come together in about the same fashion. Almost two decades later, the house looks finished from the outside, but there are significant gaps. The interior finish work — closet and cabinet doors, trim work, finished floors — all still incomplete. And there were parts that were finished too hastily and needed (and in some cases still need) to be redone the right way.

The place is certainly unique ... which we love. But that uniqueness takes away much of the ease of standard application. And the 52-acre hilltop that ensures our privacy comes at the expense of a steep, two-thousand-foot driveway that constantly needs to be maintained. It eats front ends, gives non-4-wheel-drive visitors a hike they're often not up to, and during particularly bad winters effectively maroons us in a tundra-like oasis.

But land we did get. And privacy. A view of nothing but trees, distant hills, and sky. There are resident hawks and owls, wild turkeys, fox, coyotes, bobcat, fishers, a million mice, a zillion ticks. No bar-b-cue smoke, no noisy neighbors. And my kids got a home. A little late, but some of them might say it's come in handy from time to time, even though their ideas of a desirable place to live have turned out to be very different from mine.

Would we build another house? Nobody's that crazy.

Would we have done it in the first place if we'd known then what we know now? Of course. Because we wouldn't have believed a word of it. Well ... I take that back. *I* wouldn't have believed a word. Art would have. And when I think back, I'm pretty sure he had a pile of misgivings that he simply decided to keep to himself. Because my energy for the plan was so high, and he's never quite been able to bring himself to stick pins in my ideas of what's possible. I was entranced by possibilities back then. It was the sting of reality I was trying to escape.

Would I exchange the experiences for others less hard, less overwhelming? Actually, no. Because building a house is a little like running a marathon. It hurts like hell while you're doing it, but once it's finished and you see that you've survived, there's a particularly satisfying sense of accomplishment and an undeniable elation that lasts a long long time.

Of course, it's always a good idea to *train* for a marathon, a good idea to examine the demands that will be put upon you, assess your ability to meet those demands, assess the willingness of your spirit to stay the course. We didn't do any of that, just grabbed a number and started to run. Maybe we were afraid to ask the hard questions because we knew what the answers would be, or maybe the answers didn't matter because everything we'd always counted on was already so out of focus.

We started out barely knowing a 2x4 from a six-penny nail. We didn't know about foundation footings or weight-bearing walls or rafter tie-downs or vent stacks, hadn't ever heard of a termite shield or a ridge board or a cripple stud. A joist? Isn't that something knights on horses did? Sleepers, sonotubes, soffits, stringers. Thermal mass, toenailing, Tyvek?

Up to that point, the closest I'd come to anything electric was plugging blenders and hair dryers into outlets, so if someone had told me I'd end up running five hundred feet of Romex, I wouldn't have known what they were talking about. If they'd said I'd wire a hundred outlets, I'd have said, "Not on your life," since I didn't know a hot wire from a circuit breaker.

But run Romex I did, and wire outlets, frame walls, build a chimney, run a backhoe, and work cement. All of it was hard, very hard. And slow, very slow. Much of what was hardest will never be seen ... a 2000-foot trench for the electric and telephone cable that reminded us every day for three months how Sisyphus must have felt. And then there was the cement for the foundation that came

Tima Smith

much too close to blowing out our home-made forms. And the old front-end loader that lost its tracks on a regular basis.

There were people who thought we were amazing, and let us know that. And people who thought we were out-of-our-minds and let us know that, too. And of course there were a thousand thousand hand-driven nails that hold the house together. We hope.

For a very long time I experienced an actual spurt of joy every time I came up the driveway and saw a house where nothing used to be. To this day I appreciate every flip of an electric switch, the hot water that comes out of the shower head, the roof that doesn't leak, the chimney that has a perfect updraft, the sun that pours in the windows and gives us passive solar heat on winter days. And the woods, the sky, the privacy, the quiet. These I like best of all. So maybe an explanation for why we abandoned reason and started this thing in the first place doesn't really matter at all. Maybe the fact that we set out together on a great adventure is explanation enough.

CHAPTER THREE

The Beginning

Art and I met in one of his writing classes at Brandeis University. Writing had always been something I did easily and well, and in the early 1980s I developed an urge to write fiction, the kind I'd been reading all my life. But when I actually sat down to do it, it didn't take more than a half-dozen false starts to tell me this was a horse of a different color, and I had absolutely no idea how to even begin. So I went to school. I signed up for a workshop, *How to Write Fiction*, at Brandeis University and took it for one semester, then another, and then two more after that. It wasn't until the third or fourth session that much of anything Professor Arthur Edelstein had to say about writing even began to make sense.

Practically everyone in the class kept coming back. Because no one learns to write effective fiction in a matter of weeks or a matter of months, and I, for one, got hooked on the process, the tiny little a-ha moments, becoming adept at the craft. It was exiting ... all of us poking our noses into something that seemed practically inscrutable, and, on the way, finding a like-minded pack to run with. It didn't matter that most of us were awful at it. We were learning together, learning how to do it, and the discovery of this thing turned a group of strangers into a group of friends, and then, miracle of miracles, some of us began to produce fiction that was actually readable.

Art maintained a certain distance from the class camaraderie. Not that he was unfriendly, just somewhat detached. So although he and I sat at the same round table one evening a week, week after week, we did little more than nod hello or goodbye. And for a long time, my expectation at the end of each session was that he

Tima Smith

would take me aside, point down the hall, and suggest that I "try something else."

During those two years, I did a lot of thinking, a lot of stretching. Trying to say something on the page demands that you understand it first in your head, that you consider carefully the small situations that make up a life, its meaning or lack of meaning, try to get closer to what existence is and how people muddle around inside it. For better or worse, fiction is a force for discovery, and not just on the page. It changed me on some basic level, maybe not for the wiser, but it did make me think about a lot of things that had been easier to ignore for a long time.

For one thing, I faced the fact that my marriage was in the final stage of a long, slow unraveling, and I told my husband that I needed time apart from him. It was awful ... for him, for me. But I was especially surprised by one particular feeling that I'd not expected. It was as though after years of constraint, I was finally able to take a full, deep breath. It was exhilarating. And at the same time, terrifying. As though I'd jumped off the track when I was eighteen, and now, at thirty-five, I was back on the train and its speed was throwing me every which way.

Christmas was not the best of holidays that year. We were trying to live separately, but together, and it wasn't working well at all. When Art announced an afternoon get-together at his house for his writing groups, I wasn't in much of a party mood, but I went, and it turned out to be lively and fun, and when I finally got in my car, I realized half-way home that I'd left my purse behind. I remember knocking on Art's door, and his answering it with my purse in hand. "I was hoping you'd notice before you got too far," he said, "if not, I was going to call you later." I took the purse, opened it, looked inside. "My whole life is in here," I said, and promptly burst into tears.

He sat me down, listened to me for an hour, hardly said anything, offered no advice, except to say that 'making a move,' as he put it, could be right or could be wrong. But that not making one could be just as much of a risk.

I was so torn up at the time, I could barely focus on the words, never mind what they meant, but now I realize he was trying to tell me that there was never a clear path ahead, no such thing as 'happily ever after.' That you ended up living with consequences no matter what choice you made.

Our relationship changed after that. He cared how I was, and I was so glad to have someone care. My writing was improving; class response was affirming; my confidence grew; and with it, an ease developed between the two of us, a kind of synergy. I found myself hooked on his sense of humor, his grace, his gentleness, and suddenly I fell in love. Very hard, very deeply, and for the first time in my life. It was amazing and foolish and inconvenient and a lifesaver. I was bumping along a hard reality and soaring at the same time. But I wasn't alone, because luckily, and for some reason I'll never quite understand, he, at the age of 55, fell in love right back.

In most ways, we were very different. I'd been mostly spoon-fed all my life, had little appetite for taking chances, leaps of faith weren't in my character; instead, I tended to slide into things — in and out of college, into marriage, into motherhood. While other nineteen-year-olds were off at Woodstock, I was home changing diapers.

In contrast, Art was a Brooklyn boy who grew up tough. He'd barely left the borough until the army shipped him off at seventeen to the Philippines. For ten years after he came home, he worked a full-time factory job while he took night courses at Brooklyn College, then Columbia. Eventually, he earned a Ph.D. in American Literature at Stanford, got married, had a son, divorced, published his work, got an advance for a novel. He was comfortable walking a different path ... as a writer, a literary critic, an anti-nuclear speaker in the '60s, a Viet Nam war critic in the '70s, a university teach-in organizer, a Civil Rights advocate. And through all that, he raised his son alone.

Tima Smith

What did we have in common? We had the same quirky sense of humor. We were vegetarians. We both had a yen to live a more rural, independent lifestyle. He had an extraordinary way of validating me, of according me a sense of permission to be myself. And he often said I knocked him straight out of his rut into a new appreciation of life. Most importantly, though, he was willing to exchange a reasonably comfortable, secure, predictable life for me, for my kids, for all our problems.

It took a year before we could really be together. A year of absurd complications and bizarre situations. My husband took off with everything that wasn't nailed down and a few things that were, and then completely disappeared. There was a threatened foreclosure on our home, multiple liens, five teenagers acting out in various ways. Not to mention the call from the Florida lawyer concerning my ex, who, it seemed, had taken some rather valuable marine real estate that didn't fully belong to him. Art kept me sane. And my writing, that kept me sane, too.

"You don't have to do this," I'd sometimes say to him. "You can go back to normal any time. I won't say I'll like it, but believe me I'll understand."

He'd just nod and smile and stick around. And then there was that one time when he stopped me before I could say it again. "If I quit you," he said, "then what? You think I could find someone who was smarter and better looking? Someone who was a better writer and had more kids? Someone with even less money?"

It was typical Art-speak. So okay, he wasn't going anywhere no matter what. And that way he had of using humor to disarm any situation was going to come in very handy, because it was going to help us through everything that was still to come.

***

With my three oldest off to college, two in New Hampshire and one enrolled in a year-long Audubon Program, I put my house on the market, and Art and I hatched a plan to find a place to live within two hours of Art's new teaching position at Radcliffe College. My house was too heavily mortgaged to keep, Art's house was too small for anything but two people, and living in the Boston area was simply too expensive. We needed something roomy but affordable, someplace new to start a life together. And we were prepared for the fact that anything we could afford was going to be a hefty drive from Cambridge and probably take a lot of work to fix up.

We drew a 60-mile radius around Boston, figuring anything under a two-hour commute was doable since Art was driving in only twice a week. Then we spent months checking out every area within that radius until we finally focused on the one that seemed to best offer what we were looking for — affordability plus rural character.

In the early 1980s, the northeast corner of Connecticut was largely undiscovered, with a population that had scarcely changed in fifty years. It was known as the 'Quiet Corner,' and most people in Boston, Providence, Worcester, even in Hartford, all cities only an hour or so away, had usually never even heard of it.

Art had wandered through the area a few years earlier and remembered it. We both liked the facts that cows seemed to outnumber cars, that people were friendly, and especially that house prices were even lower than we'd expected.

Then just as our plans were gelling, Art suffered a double knock-out punch health-wise.

First, he tore a retina. He ignored the tiny black dots he was seeing, didn't do anything about it right away, and because of his delay in seeking treatment, the most invasive kind of surgery became necessary. His eye did not heal well, and he ended up with a total loss of central vision in his left eye, no small thing for a man who made his living writing and reading. But he took it the way he took everything, stoically, and he adjusted, or at least seemed to.

Then, not long after, he got sick, very very sick.

Tima Smith

It started with a week-long headache that had him writhing in pain, a headache that not one doctor at two major Boston hospitals was able to properly diagnose. After about a week, the headache disappeared, but then other symptoms took over, and he began losing weight in an alarming way, a kind of gradual wasting away that left him, at the end of a few months, thirty pounds lighter and so weak he had to use his arms to lift his legs every time he got into a car. He didn't have the energy to drive, had to take stairs one step at a time, couldn't even lift a bag of groceries.

He barely complained, but it was more than just a physical blow. He seemed to age ten years in just a few months. Unable to do all the things he'd once taken for granted, he had to rely on me for everything — for opening jars, changing a tire, shoveling snow. It was a frustrating and frantic time until a doctor at a Boston Veterans Administration hospital finally made a correct diagnosis. Hyperthyroidism. His thyroid gland was producing too much thyroxine, and he was metabolizing at a furious rate, burning up protein, fat, carbohydrate — the reason for the rapid weight loss and general wasting. With medication, his body would stabilize and his symptoms gradually disappear, though we were told it could take a long time, that he would probably be on medication for years, not just weeks or months. But just the fact there was finally some improvement instead of continual weakening was a huge relief. And all the while, we kept moving ahead with our plans. A way of ignoring what was happening, a way to believe that things were going to be all right again, a thumb in the eye of providence.

***

We spent our weekends driving to Connecticut, looking at every new listing our agent Cheryl could find. We wanted something shabby but interesting, neglected but salvageable. We had enough money for a down payment with a little left over for renovation, and every house we looked at in our price range needed a lot of renovation. We looked at dozens of houses, but nothing even came close to piquing our interest. Months went by.

Fifty Acres, More or Less

A full year. And then one day Cheryl said on a whim, "Would you like to see a mansion that's on the market in town? Just for fun?"

"Yes," we said, "let's," because nothing else going on in our lives at that point was what you'd exactly call fun. And besides, how often did you get to tour a real mansion?

This particular mansion had once been a girl's boarding school. It had twenty-two rooms, 8200 square feet, and was in a state of genteel decay. It had been on the market for a very long time with no takers. Oil prices were sky-high and no one wanted to have to heat *that* house. But the price was unbeatable. At seventy-five thousand, it was probably the biggest, cheapest house in northeast America.

It had two wood stoves on the first floor, and the first floor alone was big enough to house an entire family. There was a rental apartment on the second floor, and on top of that a third floor, and then a fourth. And those floors, by the way? ... they were all solid walnut. The ceilings were ten-feet high; the main staircase, magnificent; and within ten minutes we were sure we'd found our house.

"You could put a grand piano on the staircase landing," Art said. As if we had one.

"Look at this kitchen." My voice echoed off the walls. "It's big enough to sit a football team."

It was all about wanting something despite our better instincts. I saw bedrooms for all six of our kids, a house that was reminiscent of the old Victorian I'd had to sell, a house everyone could come home to and bring lots of friends. It was a chance to get back something we'd lost. Home.

We wrestled with it. Should we actually *buy* it? The only reasonable thing it had going for it was its price. Otherwise, it was too big, too dilapidated, and it was on a main street with neighbors on two sides. What about those things we were looking for — privacy, peace and quiet?

"We could rent out rooms," I said. "It could actually be an income producer."

"We could close off the upper floors in the winter and still have plenty of space," Art said. "We could heat the first floor with the wood stoves. Plus the roof's practically new. And the plumbing didn't look *that* bad."

"Does the carriage house seem to be falling over?" I asked.

Art shrugged.

We chewed on it for a week and finally decided there was enough space, enough peace and quiet *inside* to make up for what it lacked outside.

We made an offer and held our breaths. Not because we thought we might not get it, but because we were so sure we would.

How could we know that after three years on the market with not one single taker, not one spark of interest, there was someone else thinking about buying it that very same weekend.

The day we made our offer, our agent went out of town for a week. Without telling us, the agent who was handling Cheryl's business for her while she was away submitted her own client's bid for the house before ours. When we didn't hear back in twenty-four hours, we called.

"Oh I'm sorry but that house already sold," we were told. "Just yesterday. Your offer was too late."

Too late?? Our offer was too late?? We couldn't believe it, and went so far as to call the owner, to tell her our offer had actually come in first and that it was even slightly higher than the one she'd accepted. But it was too late. The papers were signed and there wasn't a thing we could do about it.

In retrospect, it was probably the best thing that could have happened ... but we didn't know it then. It just seemed that *nothing* was going our way. We'd never find anything we could afford. We'd never find a house.

What were we going to have to do, we wondered, *build* one?

***

A month later, I saw an ad for fifty acres of land in Pomfret. It was at least forty-five acres more than we wanted, but it sounded lovely. A hilltop with a view, peaceful, quiet, private. And the price was low. Maybe we really *should* build a house?

Because I had to go to work the next day and we didn't want to wait, Art went off by himself to see if the land had potential, which he decided it did, and when we went together a few days later, it felt absolutely right. We parked the car at the bottom of the hill and walked up the driveway.

Along the low side of the hill, there were tall stands of red pine and spruce. "WPA, I bet," Art said, referring to FDR's works program. "They planted millions of trees in the '30s."

The high side was mainly red oak and maple, and as we neared the top, the trees thinned into a quarter-acre-or-so clearing. It was perfectly quiet except for a hawk's screech, and when I looked up, there were three of them gliding above us in wide circles.

We walked in four directions over rough paths, evidence of fairly recent lumbering. North brought us through thick woods downhill to a brook and wetlands with more woods beyond. East brought us to a stone wall after about a thousand yards, where the land dropped off sharply and there was a dynamite view through the trees of far-off purple hills and a farm with a red barn and cows moving across fields. West was a gentle slope with tangles of wild grapes, bittersweet vine, and wild rose bushes. Walking south, we found evidence of a well, a series of buried cisterns, piles of glass blocks, bricks, and other debris. Someone had been doing something up here. But what?

We spent several hours feeling it out, and then, toward the end of the afternoon, we were sitting on a log, when a loud sound I'd

Tima Smith

never heard before made us both look up toward the rear of the clearing. A buck was facing us, as surprised to see us as we were to see him. He was a deep reddish-brown and carried a huge spread of antlers. For a few seconds the three of us stared at each other, until he snorted again and then, quite simply, was gone.

"Wow," I said.

"Mmmm," Art answered.

We'd already agreed that even without a house, it was the best property we'd seen in over a year of looking, and as the afternoon faded and we walked back down the driveway, I think we both felt that even though the land didn't yet belong to us, we already belonged to it.

We decided to act fast because we didn't want to risk losing this one, too, but things went along without a hitch and before two weeks had gone by, we were landowners.

We'd never intended to sink practically every penny we had into a piece of land. But with fifty acres, more or less, we were sure we could sell off two or three parcels and get the money to build the house. "Who knows?" we told each other. "Maybe we'll even come out ahead."

Silly us.

After the fact, it was easy to see we should have investigated the land-sale possibility. But we were in way too much of a hurry. Besides, the bank that owned the land, after having repossessed it from the former owner, showed us their own subdivision map. Gave it to us, in fact. It divided the land into nine house sites, and we simply assumed that if they could do it, we could do it.

Trouble was, they *couldn't* do it. Which is why they hadn't. They just never bothered to mention that.

The fifty acres were effectively landlocked, bounded on two sides by privately-owned land, and on two sides by state-owned land. The first 700 feet of the driveway was a right-of-way granted by the State of Connecticut to the previous owner, who, from what we've heard since, had to fight very hard for it. The right-of-way was restricted to a width of twenty feet, and in order to sub-divide land, an access road had to be thirty feet wide. The state, it turned out, was absolutely unwilling to change the restrictions of the right-of-way agreement. And still is.

So much for coming out ahead.

Still, when it came right down to it, sub-dividing wasn't something we were all that anxious to do. We were land poor, yes, but at the same time, we were land rich. And the more we walked those fifty acres, the more attached we became to every one of them.

We came up with a plan. If we could get a mortgage using the land as collateral, and if we built the house ourselves as cheaply as possible, we could have a house *and* the fifty acres. We had to believe that. Because we'd jumped in with both feet. We owned fifty acres of land. And we'd spent every cent we had to buy it.

Tima Smith

CHAPTER FOUR

The Cast

Once we'd started down the road, we simply kept moving forward. The facts that Art could only function at half his usual strength, that we were operating on a financial shoe-string, that we'd never undertaken anything this foreign or complicated in our lives were factors we simply chose to ignore.

We began to plan the house and how we were going to build it.

Art was anxious to build something that was as energy-efficient as possible. He bought books on passive solar and alternative energy, wanted to make use of local mills, green lumber, second-hand building materials. We moved from Massachusetts to a rental in Connecticut, and my two youngest, Lauren and Brian, reluctantly transferred from a high school with 2000 students to one with 200. We bought an antique Case front-end loader to help with the hard stuff, and read absolutely everything we could get our hands on that had anything to do with building a house.

The first thing we had to tackle was taking apart and moving a fourteen-foot shed. It was the only structure on the entire fifty acres (aside from a bullet-ridden aqua-blue trailer), and wouldn't you know it was right smack in the middle of where we wanted the house to be. There was also a stone wall, one of dozens on the property, but this one ran straight through our future living room. So it had to be moved, too.

At that point, Art wasn't up to prying and rolling seventy-pound rocks, but he was the only one of us willing to drive the front-end loader, so that's what he did while I did the grunt work. It showed us two things: one, we worked well together. And two, when it was required, I could be stronger than I'd ever imagined.

By the time we actually started constructing, Art's strength had come back, although his eye problem impacted his depth perception and made hitting a nail a tricky thing.

Of course we knew from the beginning we weren't going to be able to carry off building a house all by ourselves. Two people. And certainly not if we expected to move in by the following winter, only eight months away. We were going to need help, and, luckily, the initial euphoria that went along with our intentions was catching. Our kids would help. And a couple of friends who had building experience, one a little, one a lot.

But Art and I started off alone in the winter of 1985.

We moved the stone wall and the shed. We sited the house, decided on a final plan, got the necessary permits.

We consulted a local builder of small energy-efficient houses, who told us that the price per square foot for building a house in northeast Connecticut at that time was about seventy-five dollars. "If you do most of the work yourselves," he said, "you can probably get that figure down to fifty."

He seemed to think fifty was a good goal to try for, but it wasn't good enough for us. The only way we could reduce the per square foot price below fifty was to take advantage of second-hand materials, so we began making trips to wrecking yards, looking for anything that was cheap and promising ... doors; sinks; electrical fixtures; windows; posts and beams. We didn't even have a foundation, but we gradually put together a pile of things that would become part of the house, many of which needed to be planned for prior to the actual building process anyway.

My oldest son Michael was attending college in Washington state, and when he came home for spring vacation, he helped us put the shed back together at the rear of the house site. Art's son, also a Michael, started making trips down from Vermont, where he taught elementary school, to help as well.

Tima Smith

Art and I had taken the shed apart carefully, saving just about every part. We stacked it all at the back of the cleared area, where we intended to put the shed back together. It included a neat stack of all the roof plywood, which was practically new and something we carefully removed so we wouldn't have to replace any of it. Except the next time we came ... maybe twenty-four hours later? ... the stack of plywood was gone.

Who took it, we never found out, but it was a kick in the pants to learn that country folk can be just as gnarly as those in the city. And it wasn't to be our last lesson, either.

Instead of investing in new plywood and shingles, we bought a roofing material called Onduline, a corrugated fiberglass product that nailed on quickly, wore well, and cost about a half as much as new plywood and shingles.

As soon as the shed was finished and we had a place for storage, we went out and bought the basic tools we'd need — a wheelbarrow, hammers, pry-bars, hand saws — along with a lock for the shed door. Could it be that the lock was perceived as an irresistible challenge? Because the very next day, we arrived to find it broken, the door wide open, and most of our tools gone. Some of them we never found; many had simply been heaved into the woods.

Again, it was dispiriting, even intimidating, but looking back, I think *we* were the ones being seen as the intruders.

Before the bank took it over, the property had been owned by a local legend, a pilot who was famous for setting his bulldozer on fire, for his plans to build a nightclub on top of the hill, for putting in a driveway that was an uphill engineering feat, and for trucking an aqua-blue 40-foot trailer all the way up the driveway to the top.

Unfortunately, he'd lost his job and the property, too, and took off owing money to practically everyone in the area. Because of him, the place had a reputation. And because the land had been abandoned for so long before we bought it, it had become fair game for anyone who lived nearby. Hunters used it, and used the trailer as a shooting gallery. Teenagers parked there. And locals had long ago made off with most of the 125 rhododendrons the pilot had planted along the driveway.

When we began storing building materials in earnest, we started leaving our old VW Squareback in the driveway to block the plywood thieves who, after all, had used a pick-up to haul it away and probably wouldn't have bothered if they'd had to carry it all the way down the hill on their backs. And the car did stop the pilferage. But then the car became an easy mark and ended up with a foreign substance in its gas tank, which put it totally out of commission after one last trip to the top of the hill.

The sabotage came to an abrupt end shortly after that. Probably, we decided, because a nearby family with several teenage sons moved away.

***

As soon as the weather turned decent in early spring, my Michael came home for the summer and brought a friend. Greg, my second oldest, also arrived. He was our ace in the hole, having worked with a construction crew during the previous summer. Plus he was willing to give as much time as he could spare. Neither Michael nor his friend Steve had building experience, but they were strong and enthusiastic, and didn't mind working hard or living rough. It was a lark to them, and their enthusiasm and energy were contagious.

Greg was good at sharing his building experience, never impatient or overbearing or patronizing. He didn't seem to mind being asked if this was a sixteen-penny nail or an eight-penny nail even if he'd already heard the question every day for a week.

My youngest son, Brian, was there as well, and being the youngest, he fell easily into taking directions. Unlike his brothers, who would both be leaving at the end of August and wouldn't be back full-time until the following spring, Brian had a decidedly direct stake in what was going on. He would be graduating from

Tima Smith

high school that spring, with plans to go to a nearby college, so he was going to be living in that still-to-be-built house, at least on weekends and school breaks.

Jennifer, my oldest daughter, was only thirty minutes away at the University of Connecticut, but arranged not to be around much while all the building hustle was going on. She'd visit occasionally, but I think she seriously doubted our sanity.

Lauren, on the other hand, my youngest, was only a high school junior. She was supremely stuck. Here was a girl who'd grown up in a relatively comfortable house in a middle-class suburban neighborhood, suddenly thrown into a tiny trailer on a hill in no-where Connecticut. Somehow she coped. She hardly ever complained. Though if she had, I'm not sure I could have helped. We were all on the same slippery slope, Art, me, and Lauren, heading into the same black hole. Although that summer, we didn't know it yet.

Art's son Michael (we call him Michael E to clear up the Michael confusion) came frequently and helped with some of the hardest work ... collecting stones for the floor, carrying cement chimney blocks up two ladders to the third floor, putting the roof together (even though he had to force himself, because, like me, he hates heights.) And there was Michael's girlfriend Grannis, who loved it up here, loved roughing it, and didn't mind spending some of her weekends carrying lumber and banging nails.

Jerry, a friend and fellow-writer, had supported himself with lots of odd jobs — painting, plastering, carpentry. The summer we started building, he was in residence on Cape Cod, finishing up a collection of short stories he was about to publish. He was always willing to drive the two hours to Connecticut when we needed help. And we needed help a lot.

Then there were Sue and Nick. Sue's strength was horticulture, and although we weren't ready to use her skills that summer, Nick was a lifesaver, a carpenter. When Nick showed up with his nailing belt and his tools, we knew we could relax for a while, because he was in charge. He'd walk around, looking things over, and then show us how to fix whatever mistakes we'd made since his last visit.

Pretty much, that was the cast. Though there were others from time to time, friends of Greg and Brian who came to help out and often were able to show us better ways of doing things. Especially Brian's friend Chris Barry, who arrived for a day and seemed to accomplish a week's worth of work. And Ray Galli, who gave one whole summer weekend to insulating the roof, no mean feat, considering it was in the high 80s and that combination of heat, sweltering humidity, and fiberglass was enough to make poor Ray itch like a flea-bitten hound dog. We thank you all.

Tima Smith

CHAPTER FIVE

What We Started With

Fifty acres, more or less. A high, beautiful piece of land with views of surrounding farms and distant hills. In one direction, you can see the highest point in Rhode Island. Quiet, private, wooded, and crisscrossed with stone walls, there's moist rich soil, some wetlands, and enough standing firewood to keep us warm forever. There's a no-longer-used railroad bed-turned-hiking trail bordering one edge — a great place to walk, run, ride horses. And then there's the northeast Connecticut fauna, largely invisible, although their passings are always evident the morning after a fresh snowfall.

A driveway ... a dirt driveway, approximately two thousand feet long, which leads up to the highest point on the hill, six-hundred-plus feet on the topographical map. The driveway was in great condition when we bought the land, nicely mounded in the center to direct rain water off into the grassy sides where a shallow trench carried it to a series of concrete cisterns set into the ground on the high side to collect rain and ground run-off and pass it through pipes running beneath the driveway and off into the woods on the low side.

Pretty quickly we discovered it was a famous driveway.

"Oh right," people would say, "the piece of land up on the hill with that nightmare of a road going in."

At least a dozen people told us they'd considered buying the land, but didn't because they wouldn't "touch that driveway with a ten foot pole."

But what did we know? Until then, our experience with driveways had been asphalt. And never longer than a hundred feet. As far as we were concerned, the only thing you ever had to do to a driveway was plow it in the winter. Besides, this driveway was in great shape, and it never occurred to us it wasn't going to stay that way. Of course, we didn't ruin it on purpose. It was out of sheer stupidity. And yes, we were both familiar with the Grand Canyon, with the theory behind its evolution. But its connection to our driveway simply never occurred to either one of us until it was much too late.

I suppose it's possible there were no torrential downpours in Pomfret from the time the driveway was built until we came along. But more likely, the cause of its ruination was the mound of dirt we piled along the edge when we were digging our utility trench. I mean, we had to put the dirt *some*place. And it took a long time to dig that trench, prep it for the electric and phone cables, and then fill it in. Three months. Which, in hindsight, was about two months too long. So that mound of dirt was there, blocking rainwater from running off the driveway from June through August.

For a while, all we knew was that the driveway was washing out. And depending on how hard it rained, the washouts could be anywhere from a few inches deep to a few feet. Sometimes it was so bad, the driveway became impassable.

"Damn rain," we'd mutter, filling in the holes with the Case loader, wondering if we were going to end up doing this every time it rained for the rest of our lives.

Not until we happened to be standing on the steepest part of the driveway in a deluge and actually *saw* the torrent of water pouring toward us did we finally figure out what was happening. Up at the top, it looked like nothing more than trickles of rain, but as the water collected and gained speed on the hill, blocked from running off by our self-made dirt damn, it turned into a river. In a heavy downpour, there was often so much water racing down the driveway, you couldn't see the gravel surface beneath.

But even if we had understood the problem sooner, what would we have done? Taken the time from the other thirty-two thousand things we had to do to move two hundred yards of dirt four feet to the *other* side of the run-off trench?

Tima Smith

By the end of the summer, when the utility lines were finally in and all the dirt was back where it belonged, we'd lost a good six inches of gravel from the driveway surface, which meant that most of the driveway was no longer higher than the earth along its sides, which in turn meant water couldn't get off even if it wanted to. The cost of resurfacing the road was about two thousand dollars. Not an option at that point, although today it would be a bargain. What we had to figure out was how to prevent it from continuing to wash away. And we had to do it fast.

There was lots of useless paraphernalia lying around. Unused cisterns; a set of concrete steps and two abandoned oil tanks from god knows where; yards of black plastic piping; and telephone poles. Some were leftovers from the pilot's failed attempt to do what we were doing, and some of it was from people who were simply too lazy to go to the dump. But the telephone poles … they gave us an idea.

With help from Jerry, who always seemed to be there for us at our worst moments, we ended up digging the telephone poles — six of them — across the steepest part of the driveway. We slanted them slightly toward the low side of the hill, set them at intervals of about fifty to sixty feet, and let the rounded top of each pole protrude from the ground a few inches. And okay, they added an uncomfortable, front end-eating bounce to the drive up and down, but they saved what was left of the driveway and acted (still do!) as water breaks, directing rainwater off the road and into the woods. All we had to do was keep the run-off path for each pole from getting too clogged with sand, gravel, and leaves.

Our driveway problems were solved! Well, most of them. Eventually, we learned that water bars further up the hill, on the less steep six or seven hundred feet were just as important, because these upper run-offs prevented a heavy rain from ever gathering enough force to dislodge the road surface. The intermittent upkeep these water bars require is worth every second spent on it.

Fifty Acres, More or Less

A cabin. The cabin wasn't there when we bought the land, but it was the first thing we built. A sort of hands-on primer on construction. We set it in the woods a bit, behind the house site.

We had to be out of our rental house by the first of June and we needed someplace to store our belongings until fall, when the house would be finished, or at least finished enough for us to move in. It's a small building, about 20x24, a simple structure with a shed roof, and we set it up on telephone poles (those handy things), a kind of pole house, because it was the cheapest, simplest, most efficient foundation we could come up with.

Jerry and Art used a gas-powered post-hole digger to dig the holes, a process you had to see to appreciate. The digger worked fine as long as it only had to churn through sand or clear loam, but neither of those things exist in Connecticut. Connecticut ground is essentially rocks, and as soon as that digger hit anything even slightly resistant, it went berserk.

Art and Jerry would be on each side of the digger, holding it while it chewed its way a few inches down into the ground, and then the blades would hit a rock and instead of the blades turning underground, the top of the digger would start to spin instead, with Art and Jerry spinning right along with it. Once or twice it spun them right off their feet.

I don't have any pictures of this. I wish I did.

Greg was there throughout the cabin building, showing us how to build a stud wall and how to frame a window, though he must have been gone at least once, because one of the second-hand windows we used went in upside down, and upside down it has stayed. But as with everything else that was to follow, there wasn't enough time to finish the cabin, though it did get finished enough to hold all our stuff and keep it dry. We never bothered to put on a door or finish the eaves or any of the interior, just piled our furniture and a hundred boxes into it and started working on the

Tima Smith

house. The two sofas in there served as sleeping quarters for whoever needed a bed.

A tent. It was a nice large tent my brother loaned us and never got back. We stuck a queen-sized mattress inside and that's where Art and I slept all summer. It was fine. In fact, it was quite fine. The weather was warm. The tent was water-tight. There were night noises to listen to while you fell asleep ... owls, dogs barking in the distance, crickets. And things we couldn't hear ... raccoons, rabbits, porcupines. And apparently there were skunks, as well. Our black Lab Lady heard all of them. Usually, she'd lift her head and growl, then settle down again. Except one night when she couldn't seem to resist doing a little more.

Lady. She and the tent are irrevocably connected. But first I have to say that she was one special dog ... assertive for a female, especially for a black Lab, unusually protective, almost aggressive, at least with strangers. She was from one of our own litters when my first husband and I were breeding field trial dogs. A dirty business, field trialing, an ego sport I was never comfortable with. And the training methods were dirty, as well — shock collars, shock prods, rough handling.

I want to say I decided to keep Lady, but mainly she decided to keep me. She was the sweetest, most affectionate puppy in the litter, and from day one she chose to attach herself to my heels. She was irresistible, and I made it clear that this was one dog who was going to be exempt from training and trialing. She was *my* dog.

Even though she only spent two years on the hill, I like to think she loved it as much as we did. Early on, she developed a perimeter she traveled every morning. She'd trot down the driveway a few hundred yards, stopping to sniff at the remnants of whatever had passed by during the night, pushing her nose into crevices in stone walls, checking out the deer paths, and covering every stray scent with her own. Then, when she was satisfied everything was as it should be, she'd come back and stand watch for the rest of the day. She was never more than ten feet away from whatever was going on, the definition of faithful.

Of course she slept in the tent with us all summer, and it was a night in early October when she managed to redefine the word 'stink.'

What I remember is Lady flying out of the tent, then a huge commotion, then her slinking back in. But mostly what I remember is the *smell*.

Oh, I'd smelled skunks before, but never this close, never this fresh, never like this. It was a smell you could taste and feel, a smell that made your stomach sick and your eyes sting and it was everywhere all at once.

"Holy shit," Art said.

"Quick," I yelled, "get out!"

The tent became instantly useless, and a day or so later, we reluctantly burned it. We pulled our mattress out of the tent and leaned it against a tree, and Art went to two all-night convenience stores, bringing back all the tomato juice on the shelves. Then we soaked what we could, including Lady and ourselves.

But this was a smell that wasn't going to disappear easily.

Michael E and Grannis, who were visiting that weekend and had been asleep in the cabin while all this was going on, listened to our story the next morning, half-amused, half-horrified, and decided Art and I needed to get off the hill for a while. They invited us out for breakfast.

"Breakfast?" I said. "We can't go into a restaurant. We stink!"

"I can't smell anything," Michael said, sniffing. He turned to Grannis, "Can you?"

She shrugged. "Well ... it's probably just because we're standing right here. Where it happened."

Tima Smith

"Yeah," Michael said, "that's why it would be good to leave for a while. Give it a chance to dissipate."

Art looked at me. "Why don't we go," he coaxed.

Breakfast was usually something we skipped or something we unwrapped out of a box. Never hot, never tasty, never inviting. And the thought of sitting down and being served something delicious was tough to resist. But even though I tried, I simply couldn't convince myself I was the only one smelling what I was smelling.

"No," I said, trying not to think about French toast, pancakes, fresh orange juice, "we can't go."

"Oh c'mon," Michael said. "It's not that bad. Really."

I shook my head.

You two go without us. We'll come some other time. That's what I expected Art to say. We'd had a rotten night. I was tired and I was miserable and I wanted him to stay and be miserable right along with me.

But that's not what he said. Instead, he turned to me. "Sure you won't come?"

I just looked at him. He was *going*? He actually intended to leave me here all by myself??

It was a short answer: yes. And off they went. For pancakes with syrup, for eggs and buttered toast, for good hot coffee, leaving me — virtuous, skunky me — to make do with a couple of lousy breakfast bars.

I watched Michael's car disappear down the driveway.

Lady, who'd already forgotten that anything had happened at all, wagged her tail at me, glad that I'd stayed behind to keep her company.

"This is all your fault," I told her.

She wagged her tail harder.

I tried to find something useful to do, but I was feeling too sorry for myself, and suddenly, in a much shorter time than I'd expected, Michael's car was coming back up the driveway.

"Well, that was a bad idea," Art said, getting out of the car.

I started feeling instantly better.

Grannis shook her head. "You should have seen the looks we got."

"He practically cleared the whole place out," Michael said. "You guys really do stink."

"Well ... at least I hope you all enjoyed your breakfast," I said, not meaning a word of it.

Art shook his head. "No breakfast," he said. "We decided the best thing was to get up and leave."

Grannis laughed. "What he means is the waitress brought our menus and never came back for the order."

For the next few days, we took as many cold showers as we could stand and waited for what was left of the smell to wear off.

Our tent was gone. So we moved into the cabin.

A forty-foot aqua-blue trailer. It was probably a fine trailer at one time and would have been an adequate place to live while we were building if it hadn't been shot up, axed, smashed, splintered, and generally vandalized to smithereens. The floor was torn up, the ceiling torn down, the windows torn out. The toilet was in pieces, the furniture had been pulled out of the walls, the refrigerator was ten feet away in the woods. Even the carpet was shredded. The exterior had been used as target practice for guns and machetes. And we could only guess why.

We cleaned out one end so we could store a few things inside, but mainly it was an eyesore until we finally had enough time to peel all the aluminum off the exterior, sell it, deconstruct the rest, burn the wood, and haul what was left to the dump. One thing I

Tima Smith

know for sure — there were generations of mice inhabiting that thing. Because as we tore it down, they all moved into our house.

An outhouse. It was the best thing on the hill. Roomy, well-built, and waterproof. We used it for a long long time. Long enough for the novelty to wear off. Long enough so that when one of our earthy-crunchy friends came to visit and said, "Can you tell me why anyone needs more than this?" I wanted to kill her. But instead of committing mayhem, I simply pointed out that it was July, that it was the middle of the day, and the sun was shining. "Come back in February," I said, "at 2 A.M., when it's seventeen degrees below zero and you have the runs." Then we both laughed a little, like it was almost a joke.

I wondered what she would have done if she'd been the one sitting there when the meter reader came, read the meter, and then turned to leave, giving him a direct eye-shot of the outhouse door. It wouldn't have been so bad except the outhouse door wouldn't close because there was too much ice built up on the ground. My friend probably would have enjoyed it about as much as I did.

Usually, though, it was a fairly private outhouse. It was well-lit, it was well-ventilated, and relatively comfortable; still, the day I pushed it over onto its side and whacked it to pieces with a maul was a very very good day.

A well. It had been one of the selling points, that there was a well already drilled. And there *was* a metal casing for a well pump sticking up out of the ground. But all in all, the well, or at least what we assumed was the well, was a great and persistent mystery.

For one thing, the metal casing didn't have a top. It was just an open casing. Though if you stuck a 2x4 down inside, the 2x4 only went down about two feet and hit an obstruction.

This, we were told, was a bad sign. Along with all the pieces of black plastic well pipe lying around here and there. All of it was a very bad sign. Bad sign of what? Nobody was sure. They were just sure it was very very bad.

An old Case front-end loader. Art decided we needed the Case because he knew we were going to be moving and hauling and lifting far more than we were capable of. It was an old machine, but it was within our budget. Besides, it ran well and looked absolutely indestructible.

Trouble is, it had one gigantic problem. The tracks kept falling off.

We'd chosen a tracked vehicle, as opposed to one with wheels, because of the slope of our land. We needed something that could crawl up and down those slopes safely and surely, and the tracks were phenomenal for this. But not when they slipped off the sprockets and idler wheels and ended up on the ground. And in the beginning, before we understood what was happening, they *always* ended up on the ground.

You'd be merrily working along, and all of a sudden — clunk — you'd slip a track. They were probably the wrong tracks for the machine or maybe the parts that were supposed to hold them on were missing. But at the time, we thought it was us. You could be going forwards, backwards, turning right, turning left, when suddenly, and for no apparent reason, you were going nowhere at all. Sometimes it was the right track, sometimes the left, and on particularly bad days, it was both at the same time.

The first time it happened, it took an assortment of pry bars, a six-foot metal pipe, a sledgehammer, and five hours to get one track back on. And even though Art eventually figured out a method of using the loader's own weight to help the process, working a four-hundred-pound steel track back into place with levers and sledges usually ruined our moods along with most of an afternoon.

Books. A whole library of them. On wiring, plumbing, framing, chimneys, solar heat, roofs, masonry. Mainly, we relied on three. One by Alex Wade called *A Design and Construction*

Tima Smith

Handbook for Energy-Saving Houses. One by Sam Clark called *Designing and Building Your Own House Your Own Way* and another by Peter Hotton called *So You Want To Build A House*. We chose a passive solar design we liked from Wade's book and then adapted it. But everything was right there in black and white, all the information we needed. All we had to do was absorb it.

    Tools. We bought a table saw, a circular saw, and a jigsaw and left them all in their boxes until we finally had electricity. We already had an assortment of hand saws, hammers, levels, squares, and tape measures. We bought a speed square, a line level, and three ladders of various lengths. We rented big equipment as we needed it.

    A budget. A very narrow one. We'd spent practically all our money buying the land. Once we moved to Connecticut, I wasn't working, only occasionally selling stories. Art was teaching, but only part-time. To keep the project moving and hit our deadline, we needed to build full-time, but doing it full-time meant we weren't bringing in much income. In the beginning, we thought this would be very temporary.

    Because we owned the land outright, we were able to get a building loan, and things would have worked out better if our original time estimates hadn't been so far off. Ending up a year behind threw things into financial chaos, and we ended up living off the building money and having to cut our house expenses way beyond the bone. We were trying to build the house for less than half of what we'd been told it would cost us per square foot doing all the work ourselves. And we may actually have done it. We may actually have built the thing for about twenty dollars a square foot. But we'll never know because we've never had the energy to sit down and figure it out. Besides, all our receipts, which for some reason we kept in the aqua trailer, disintegrated one night in a nor'easter.

A shower. It was one of the first things I built all by myself. I made it out of scraps and it looked it. It had no door, I wasn't experienced enough for that, but I set it in front of an evergreen, with the opening facing the tree, and strung a sun shower at the top, a black rubber bladder that held enough water to wet yourself once and then rinse almost all the soap and shampoo off. The sun heated the water in the bag to a fairly comfortable temperature, and, granted, we didn't take nearly as many showers as we would under normal circumstances, but as long as the temperature stayed within a reasonable range, we showered often enough to stay sociable.

Tima Smith

PHOTOGRAPHS (following)

First Page: The Beginning

Top Left: Greg (left) and Michael during the cabin construction
Top Right: Tima cutting boards
Middle Left: Art digging the foundation
Middle Right: Our foundation
Bottom Left: Greg and Steve getting the tracks back on the Case
Bottom Right: The electric and phone cables in the trench from hell

Second Page: The House Goes Up

Top Left: The first floor with the carved salvage-yard posts
Top Right: Art nailing
Bottom Left: Art nailing, with Brian watching
Bottom Right: Art and Michael E pretending to do something

Third Page: ...And Up

Top Left: How far along we were when winter caught us
Top Right: Greg standing on top of the second floor
Middle Left: Art wishing he were somewhere warm
Middle Right: Our view of the highest spot in Rhode Island
Bottom Left: The first floor takes shape around our bright blue pressure tank (holding our water)
Bottom Right: Entertaining with the ubiquitous mess outside

Fifty Acres, More or Less

Fourth Page: Will It Ever Be Completely Finished?

Top Left: Greg waiting for the next roof rafter and acting nonchalant
Top Right: One side of the roof fully raftered
Middle Left: Art on the peak. Note the flimsy staging
Bottom Left: Siding finished. No mudroom yet
Bottom Right: Art 30 feet off the ground on the ladder held by the tractor bucket

Fifth Page: Moving In

Top Left: Art and Tima and Lady using our new kitchen counter
Top Right: Almost a house
Middle Left: Tima in the kitchen
Middle Right: A house
Bottom Left: Our second-hand and very inexpensive living room windows
Bottom Right: Our bedroom

Sixth Page: The Interior Today

Top Left: Living Room, looking east toward stairs and porch beyond
Top Right: Living Room, looking west
Middle Left: Room at top of first-floor stairs
Middle Right: Through hallway to porch, with stone floor
Bottom Left: Living Room, looking east toward deck and view
Bottom Right: Living Room, looking east toward deck

Tima Smith

Seventh Page: Kitchen Today and, Finally, a Porch

Top Left: Same view of kitchen as on fifth page, but slightly improved
Top Right: Starting the porch, with Emma's help
Middle Left: Porch roof rafters
Middle Right: The porch takes shape
Bottom Left: Greg, wondering if his mother will ever stop building things
Bottom Right: Mostly finished and waiting for screening after winter is over

Tima Smith

Fifty Acres, More or Less

Tima Smith

Fifty Acres, More or Less

Tima Smith

Fifty Acres, More or Less

51

CHAPTER SIX

Going Underground –

When we decided to build, *build* was the only concept we understood. It meant going up, as in the house is *going up.* The only visions we had were of walls and windows, doors and rooms. The concepts we didn't have were of things like foundations, utilities, septic systems. Hard things. The things nobody ever sees.

In March, I stood on the spot where we'd decided to put the house and imagined what it would some day be like. Here, I was standing in the living room. Over here, I was in the kitchen. And right here would be the first floor bathroom. Five months later, I stood on the same spots and saw pretty much what I'd seen in March. Nothing.

Except now there was a septic system over there. But you couldn't see it. And the utilities were in, but you couldn't see them either, except for a temporary meter on a board sticking out of the ground. And there was a rectangular frame of concrete sticking up above the ground a foot or so, the top of the foundation. But that was it.

"So where's this house you've been building?" people would say, grinning. They didn't realize that after five months of hell, saying something like that was almost like waving a red flag in front of a bull. Most of the time, we managed to grin back. But it wasn't easy.

We knew what was buried there. A thousand dollar well pump. The unconventional foundation forms we'd designed and built ourselves, and which *almost* worked perfectly. Forty-five yards of concrete we had to puddle and screed and pray wouldn't set before we'd done everything that was necessary to do to it. Two thousand feet of electric and phone line. Oh, and let's not forget the three thousand dollar engineered septic system.

We'd spent four months' worth of ten and twelve-hour days, seven days a week, and it seemed all that work should be a whole lot more visible than it was.

Water –

Back when our expectations were as high as our excitement, the first thing we decided to do was get the well functioning, even though we weren't sure it *could* function. In addition to the ten thousand dollar driveway, the eccentric pilot had sunk a six-hundred-foot well before disappearing. Which was good. The well, I mean, not the disappearing. But there was also the distinct possibility that the well was *bad*.

For those of you who know nothing at all about wells, a well generally consists of a metal casing about six inches in diameter which protrudes two feet above ground level and reaches down into a water supply (our water was about two hundred feet down.) A cylindrical pump is lowered to below the water level inside that casing, and attached to the top of the pump is 2" diameter rigid plastic hose which rises to just below the frost line (4' in this case), where it makes a right-angle turn toward the house, runs through the foundation wall, and then into a pressure tank which always holds a certain minimum water supply. To keep debris, chipmunks, and small puppies from falling down the well casing, it's topped with a bolted-on metal cap.

The reason our well was suspect is that it was missing its cap. Plus there was an obstruction about two or three feet down inside the casing that no one could figure out.

Tima Smith

Three well-drillers came out to look at it and all they could suggest was drilling a new well. "It's fishy," they said, "all this plastic pipe lying around, that blockage in the casing, no cap. They're all bad signs. Very very bad signs."

"What do you think is blocking the pipe?" we asked.

They shrugged.

"Who knows what's down inside there," one well-driller said, "but whatever it is, it's probably ruined the well. If I were you, I'd drill a new one."

Oh, and the new well…? That was going to cost anywhere from four to eight thousand dollars. Maybe more.

Problem: we didn't *have* four to eight thousand dollars (or maybe more) to spend on a new well. We needed to resuscitate the well we had.

One day I got out the phone book and tried one more call. "Oh right," the man from Clearwater Well Drilling said, "that land the pilot used to own."

I explained the problem, anticipating consternation, confusion, the usual questions.

"Well, sure," the Clearwater man said, "that's the well cap you're hitting. Someone must'a drove it down inside the casing."

"Why would someone do that?" I asked.

I could see him shrug over the phone. "Vandalism. Kids probably."

He told me he could fix it by digging down around the casing to expose several more feet of the pipe and then cut it off below the jam. "Then you weld on a new piece'a pipe," he said, "bolt on a new cap. "Be good as new. Bet there's a good one-amp pump still down inside there, too. In fact, there's a good chance it'll even work."

A-ha. Truly amazing. The man was a visionary. How else to explain it? He'd figured out over the phone what people who had physically *looked* at it, *tapped* on it, *mused* over it, couldn't. He even envisioned the size of the pump still inside.

As it turned out, we did not hire him. Somehow it seemed a little risky, doing business with the person who'd installed the whole thing in the first place, then damaged it when he didn't get his money, *and* thought you weren't smart enough to figure that out for yourself.

But at least he'd given us a free diagnostic service. The least he could do, we decided. It turned out that his prediction about the pump still being good was wrong, so we had to install a new one. But Ernie, the man we hired to actually carry it all out, did a great job and didn't charge anywhere near the thousand dollars the visionary was going to charge.

So we had water. Or at least the potential for water. As soon as we had electricity to spark the new pump, *then* we'd have water. In the meantime, it was summer, and it wasn't such a bad walk downhill to another well we'd found on the property. This, a shallow dug well with a stone enclosure, which, we found out later, had once served the trains that stopped to fill up on the now-defunct rail bed, and also supplied two farms on the other side of the tracks. You had to lower a pail and you couldn't drink from it because it was open to contamination, but you could shower with it, wash your hands and face with it, dunk your head in it after you'd carried your full pail back up through the woods and felt like you were going to die.

Now all we needed before we could start *building* was a foundation, a septic system, and electricity. Easy. What did we know?

We rented a backhoe.

Power –

We did a lot of research on this aspect of the project. Ideally, we preferred not to be on the electric grid, and because getting power to the top of the hill was going to cost several thousand dollars, we wanted to investigate all other options. But there were few and, surprisingly, they made hooking up to the grid sound like a bargain.

While he was in Boston one day, Art had a conversation with a rep from a company who manufactured photo-voltaic cells. It seemed like such a reasonable thing to do, use the sun to power one's energy needs.

"So?" I asked, when Art got back. "Is it doable?"

"Well, that depends on what you mean by doable," he said, exercising his tendency to be enigmatic

"Doable," I said, "you know ... as in, can we do it or not?"

First he made sure he had my full attention, then he said, "For the same six thousand dollars the electric company's going to charge — for six *thousand* dollars — we can get enough photo-voltaic wattage to power..." he held up a finger, "approximately one light bulb."

"Very funny," I said.

But he wasn't being funny.

It seemed that photo-voltaic technology wasn't being even vaguely promoted by private or governmental funding as a potentially viable source of alternative energy. It was this way in 1986 and it was going to stay that way for a very long time.

So there went a fair degree of our self-sufficiency.

There was always the idea of using a generator, but that was going to require a direct current system, which meant alternative and more expensive appliances and a minimum of available power. Plus a generator is a noisy beast.

So we called the electric company and signed their contract.

But what we thought was a reasonable desire — to have electricity — turned out not only to be unreasonable, but diabolic.

Its spawn? The trench from hell.

Fifty Acres, More or Less

The purpose of the trench from hell was to hold the electric cable and the phone cable. It was approximately two thousand feet from the town road to the top of the hill, a thousand of which was straight up, well ... not *straight* up, but *up*.

The trench was necessary because the right-of-way leading to our property specified underground utilities, which was fine with us. No ugly poles and lines messing up the pristine forest. And aside from the sheer length of it, it didn't sound that complicated. Dig a trench three feet deep, throw in some sand, throw in the electric and phone lines, add more sand, then fill in the trench. One, two, three.

At least that's what the people at the phone company said. They weren't concerned about their phone cable in the least. It was a quarter-inch in diameter with no heavy-duty coating, covering, or protection. Maybe they put a spell on it before it left the factory that made it indestructible.

On the *other* hand, the electric cable apparently had no such spell. Even though it was four inches in diameter, with a rugged black rubber coating surrounded by a spiral of steel wire, the electric company's cable turned out to be a strangely delicate thing.

And because it was a delicate thing, the bottom of the trench it was to lie in had to be filled with six inches of soft sand unsullied by pebbles or rough sharp objects of any kind before the electric company would lay their cable upon it. Then once it was laid, it had to be covered with six more inches of unsullied sand before the trench could be refilled. And even then, the trench couldn't be filled with dirt containing rocks or stones or pebbles. Because the cable could, in fact, be completely put out of commission by a pebble *this* (hold your fingers a fraction of an inch apart here) big. I learned this from an electric company inspector who came to look at the trench one day just prior to installation.

He chose to come one morning after a torrential rain (it was the second or third of several torrential rains that August) and, of

Tima Smith

course, after the six inches of sand we'd just finished spreading in the trench the day before had all washed downhill and disappeared. This was the second or third time in a month we'd spread the sand, and the second or third time it had washed away.

It seemed to me that one would expect to find the sand collected in the trench at the bottom of the hill so that at least some of it could be redistributed. But it wasn't there. It simply vanished. All in all, it simply vanished *four* times.

Generally it took two days to fill the trench with six inches of sand and less than a half hour for the rain to make it disappear. And truly I wanted nothing more that day the inspector showed up than to make *him* disappear right along with all that stupid sand.

It had been a particularly bad morning. Not only had the rain washed the sand out of the trench, but it had washed out portions of the driveway, as well, making it, essentially, unusable. There were a half-dozen two foot deep gullies that needed to be filled before we could do anything about the trench, but before we could do anything about the driveway, we needed to get the tracks back on the Case, because they'd fallen off first thing. *Both* of them.

So this was the scenario: the driveway was impassable; the Case had slipped both its tracks; there was no sand in our newly-sanded trench; and there came the electric inspector for an inspection.

Art and I had had words. With everything that had happened that morning, if we hadn't had words, we'd probably have experienced spontaneous canonization on the spot.

I, for one, was suffering from transference. I was depressed, frustrated, and just plain mad. But in our circumstances, it was often tough to find something to be specifically mad *at*. It was our situation that kept kicking us in the rear. So I decided to get mad at the Case. I didn't much like it anyway.

Because Art approached everything with a much more well-defined since of logic than I, he might get annoyed when the tracks

Fifty Acres, More or Less

fell off, but he wouldn't get *mad* at the machine. He'd just fix it. Because he never lost sight of the fact that we needed the beast.

I, on the other hand, wanted to show it exactly what I thought of it by letting it sit there until it turned into a pile of rust. Wouldn't *that* serve it right! And because Art was being so damn rational about the whole thing, I got mad at him, too.

I started filling in the wash-outs with a shovel, a hopeless process. But I wanted the Case to disappear. I never wanted to see it again, hear it again, see those stupid tracks come off again.

"We need to get the tracks back on," Art said. "Why are you wasting your time? It'll take all day to fix the road by hand."

"It'll take all day to get those damn tracks back on, too," I said. "Then it will take another whole day to fix them when they come off again! *You* get the tracks back on if that's what you want to do. At least I'll get the road fixed!"

So Art left me on the road and hiked up to the top of the hill to get all the track-replacing gear. I shoveled pitiful amounts of dirt into the washouts knowing he was right, knowing this *was* going to take all day. But then what didn't? *Everything* took all day! And it looked like everything was going to take all day for the rest of our lives!

So that's the kind of awful, nasty, fed-up, don't-you-dare-look-at-me-the-wrong-way mood I was in when the electric company inspector arrived.

I remember he looked very clean, very neat. Like someone who lived in very close proximity to a shower and a washing machine. That alone made me dislike him. He walked the trench, shaking his head a lot and then proceeded to give me a lecture. "Do you realize," he said, "that a tiny pebble, a pebble *this* big can knock out the entire cable?" He indicated something the size of a pin. Then he pointed in the direction of the trench. "This trench is not properly prepared. There are *stones* in it. There's no bed of sand. And if the trench is not properly prepared, we, the electric company, cannot guarantee the installation! *You* will have to be responsible for any problems you encounter in the future!"

Normally, I hate confrontation. But there was nothing remotely normal about that morning. Nothing remotely normal about that situation. "A pebble?" I said. Could I have shrieked it? "You're telling me you make something for an underground installation that can be put out of commission by a *pebble*??"

"Well," he said, backing away, "maybe not a *pebble* exactly."

Now on the other hand, the first part of that trench, the digging part, was almost fun. I'd grown up during a time when girls played with girl stuff, and although I couldn't remember ever finding backhoes fascinating, they, in fact, are. They make noise, they swivel, they lurch, they hold amazing amounts of dirt, they move immovable boulders. And they make you feel very very empowered. They also require manual dexterity, even some finesse. On the negative side, on a slope, they often feel as though they're going to tip over, which I didn't like at all.

We started digging the trench at the beginning of April. We were supposed to have electricity and a foundation by the beginning of May. But of course we also thought we were going to have the whole house framed and roofed by the first of July. And we were still certain we'd be inside the house by the end of September. It wouldn't be finished, that we knew, but it would be finished enough to keep us dry. And by December there'd be a Christmas tree in a corner of the living room and a wood stove blazing away, hot meals, showers, and lots of windows to sit by and watch the snow sifting down out of a low gray sky.

What really happened is that they didn't lay the cable until the end of August, and we didn't start framing the house until after Labor Day.

Fifty Acres, More or Less

House Site –

Siting the house was the first major decision Art and I made. It was also our first major disagreement. It set a precedent for making decisions that continued throughout the whole project; i.e., decisions were always going to take twenty times longer than they should, unless we were in absolute one hundred per cent agreement right off the bat. Which we hardly ever were.

It always went this way: we had to decide on something — say, on what color to paint the trees. I would say blue, not even considering that Art might not agree. He'd say yellow. And he had a way of saying it that made *my* choice seem like a kind of mental aberration. (This attitude thing worked in both directions, by the way.) So we'd get into a discussion cum argument over it, which dealt not only with the surface thing about what color the trees should be, but with something subliminal that was all about ego and pride and power. And since, especially in the beginning before we began to handle things better, each of us believed he/she was totally right and the other totally wrong, the discussion cum argument could go on and on, until we dropped the whole thing or grabbed gloves and struck each other across the face.

To our credit, we never got to the striking point. After a while, we tended to drop a matter that seemed resistant to negotiation. Of course, we knew we'd have to deal with it sooner or later, but later usually seemed wiser at a certain point.

Besides, I was thinking, Art's bound to see the light and change his mind. Was Art thinking the same thing?

The decision would go on a shelf, perhaps more than once, until one of us managed to convince the other, or one of us simply gave in (usually Art). So a decision that was supposed to be made on a Monday, got shelved until Wednesday, or the following Friday, or maybe even a week from Friday. It meant self-inflicted delays, in addition to all the other kind.

Tima Smith

    But as far as siting the house went, I wanted the house to sit at the back of the cleared flat area on top of the hill. Art thought that was ridiculous. He wanted to put it right at the edge of the downslope so that from inside the house you'd get a feeling of the hill's height.

    "What's the use of living on a hill," he said, "if you don't take advantage of it? If you're going to set the house way back there, we might as well build it down at the bottom."

    I tried picturing the house where he wanted to put it, and got a pretty good idea of why I didn't want it there. It was a personality thing. And a stomach roll thing. I didn't like being on the leading edge of anything. I liked being in the background. If Art had had his way ... if he'd had the engineering know-how or the money or both, and, oh right, if *I* hadn't been there, he'd have set the house not only *at* the edge, but directly *into* the side of the hill. So that if you slipped while you were taking out the garbage, you'd roll several hundred feet until you were stopped by a tree.

    Luckily, he didn't have the know-how or the money, and I *was* there, and after several days of *discussion* we reached our first compromise. We set the house closer to the front slope, but far enough back so I wouldn't gasp every time I looked out a window.

    Once *that* was out of the way, we had to set up the exact dimensions of the foundation, and since this was before the days of laser tools, we discovered the function of batter boards.

    Batter boards are stakes driven into the ground to mark the corners of the house. They aren't actually *at* the corners though, or else they'd be in the way of the digging. They're about fifteen feet *back* from the actual corners.

    Picture this. Each actual corner is the top of a pyramid lying on its side with its base pointing away from the foundation. At the two corners of the pyramid's base, you drive two upright 2x3 stakes set three feet apart into the ground. Each set of stakes is joined by a horizontal 1x4, and a nail sticks up dead center atop that 1x4. For a standard square or rectangular foundation, there'll be eight batter boards, two at each corner.

By running a taut string from the nail on each batter board to its counterpart at the adjacent corner, you create a virtual foundation of strings, and where those strings touch are the *actual* corners of your house.

The actual corners need to be perfectly square or else framing will be a nightmare and you'll end up with a living room that measures sixteen feet at one end and fourteen and a half at the other.

Setting up batter boards is one of those rare moments when, for some people at least, two semesters of geometry actually come in handy. I wasn't one of them. I still had to learn that it wasn't sixteen feet and three little marks, but sixteen feet and 3/16 of an inch. Art, on the other hand, not only remembered his geometry, but understood it perfectly and could use it. He didn't even need a pencil and paper, he could do the figuring in his head.

The way you square the corners of your house is to measure the diagonals of your taut string foundation. If the diagonals are equal, then your corners are square. Ours weren't. They hardly ever are. It's something you have to fiddle with. For instance, we'd measure one diagonal at 475 9/16 inches, the other at 482 7/8 inches. Art would stand there staring off into space while his mental computer kicked in. "That line on that batter board has to be moved one and seven-eighth inches to the left," he'd say, "and the other line, three-quarters of an inch to the right." Or something like that. And he was right. Every time. It was damn impressive.

It took a couple of days to build and set up the batter boards, and an afternoon to square the corners, and then we jumped inside and tried visualizing the first floor.

Essentially, it was one large area with interior walls for the bathroom and utility room only. We marked off the kitchen, the

Tima Smith

entryway, the dining area, the living area, the stairs to the second floor, and the utility room where the well pipe was already in place.

It was spring. We were taking an early but significant step in our building process. *This* was going to be where our house would stand. It was exciting. And I remember feeling almost giddy with the expectation of actually beginning to *build!*

Art shook his head. "It's too small."

My giddiness vanished. "What do you mean, 'too small!'"

Art had lived in a tiny converted summer camp on a pond for twenty years. He loved the area, the pond, but he was dead-set against our house having the cramped feeling he'd lived with there.

"Just a few feet in each direction," he said, "will make a big difference. And it's an easy thing to do now."

"Easy?" I said, looking at the batter boards, the strings, thinking of two days lost.

But he was convinced, and I knew he had an ability which I did not, to visualize spatially. I could only see things that were concrete. So we took down the batter boards, spent another day setting them up again to the bigger dimensions, and then another day squaring the corners and making sure the well pipe still came up inside the utility room instead of the hallway.

When we were done, we knew where our house was going to go exactly. It was a heady moment.

We'd cleared the site, moved a stone wall, moved a shed, straightened out the well problem.

It was the beginning of everything, and we were invincible.

Fifty Acres, More or Less

I

Throughout the two years we were literally trying to get a roof over our heads, I fell asleep within seconds every night. All the hard physical work we were doing all day, every day, usually put us in bed by nine o'clock. We were simply exhausted at the end of each day. But there were some nights, a few, when, at least for me, sleep held off for a while and I would lie there listening to the sounds in the woods ... owls hooting, raccoons scrapping, tree frogs ... I didn't think about the house, because that already consumed my days ... but sometimes what I thought about was the why of the house, how it came to be and how I came to be there ... and how a life that seemed outwardly stable could, in a remarkably short period of time, come to bear very little likeness to what it once was.

CHAPTER SEVEN

The Foundation –

People who decide to build their own house should have an occasional success. It should be an early success so there'll be inspiration enough to keep going. And it shouldn't be a merely satisfactory success; it should be an *extremely* satisfactory success. Something to gloat over.

When it comes to building your own house, gloating isn't dangerous, it's therapeutic, and the reason it isn't dangerous, the reason you never have to worry about getting cocky or smug is that you have more than enough horrifying experiences to make sure cockiness doesn't even begin to gain a toehold.

We were lucky to have one early, gloat-inducing success, which happened while we were still enduring the trench from hell, and came close to balancing out the trench's horrors. It was our foundation.

Foundations are things you need to get out of the way before you can get to the stuff you're really after. Like shopping for the ingredients before you can make that dynamite chocolate mousse or having to learn to do a 360-degree roll before you can go sea kayaking.

The problem is, it's the preliminaries that tend to foul things up. You know … the store's out of bittersweet chocolate or you can only manage a 180-degree roll and end up hanging upside down from the kayak until someone happens to notice you've been underwater for a long time.

People don't set out to dig a foundation. They set out to build a house, and then, a little ways into it, they realize they can't get one without the other, that the house has to sit on something, be anchored to something. And furthermore, they discover that 'something' has to conform to certain codes so it won't crack or heave or sink or allow the house to blow off during a hurricane.

It was a hard thing to get excited over, the foundation. It was a hunk of concrete, ugly, essentially colorless, all right-angles and rough surfaces. And it was going to take time, time we wanted to be putting into our *house*, not into something that was going to be 99% covered as soon as it was finished.

Of course, we knew there were people who didn't see foundations that way, people who got paid to focus all their attention on them. Foundation crews who had knowledge, experience, and the right equipment. It didn't bother them one bit that their work disappeared before they were out of the driveway. But hiring a foundation crew was going to cost too much and, anyway, they were all too busy to come when we needed them. Plus they moved too much earth, and we wanted to be foundation minimalists.

Okay, we'd build it ourselves.

We weren't going to have a basement, just a slab, so all we needed was a perimeter trench full of concrete, four simple concrete walls to hold up the house. How hard could that be?

Theoretically, if you're not going to have a basement, you should be able to dig a ten-inch wide trench into previously undisturbed earth exactly where you want to build the exterior walls of your house, fill those trenches with concrete and start building. However, it doesn't work that way. The walls of the foundation have to sit on something called a footing. The footing gives the foundation walls stability. The footing needs to be as deep top to bottom as the foundation walls are wide, and twice as wide as the foundation walls are thick, which means the entire trench has to be as wide as the footing. So there go your undisturbed earth walls for supporting the foundation.

People who were paid to make foundations had forms they set into the overly wide trench on top of the footing. These forms held

Tima Smith

a concrete pour, and once the pour was set, the foundation people hopped into the overly wide trench, took out their forms, and went home. We didn't have forms, but we realized we were going to need them. We didn't want to rent them because that cost too much money. And it seemed inefficient to build forms we'd never use again.

We wondered: What if we could come up with something minimal but adequate that we could leave in the ground? We decided to think about it while we dug the foundation trench.

The fact that we were putting in a foundation elicited one truism and one cautionary remark from just about everyone we came in contact with. The truism had to do with the fact that nobody puts in their own foundation. "You're putting in your own foundation?" people would say. "Nobody puts in their own foundation!" The cautionary remark had to do with ledge. "Hope you don't run into ledge." "Bet you'll hit ledge." "Watch out for ledge."

That last one made it sound as though ledge was something you could avoid if you were smart enough or quick enough or had some kind of detector that warned you it was approaching.

It had never occurred to us that we couldn't put in our own foundation and it had never occurred to us that we might hit ledge. We weren't even sure what ledge was. And if we did hit it, we weren't sure what kind of problem it would cause. And, of course, we never asked any of these 'ledge warners' the question, "Why?" because that would have seemed too much like admitting we didn't know what we were doing. We wanted to keep that to ourselves as much as possible.

I've looked up ledge since then, and it's defined as a layer or mass of rock beneath the ground. One of our building books thought ledge was fine, that if you hit it, you were finished digging, because it would hold up your house even better than concrete.

Still, the warnings were worrisome enough to have us saying to each other every morning, "Hope we don't hit ledge today."

As it turned out, the digging was a fairly problem-free experience, except for a concussion and the fact that we broke the first backhoe we rented. The problem with the backhoe was nothing serious, just a hose that couldn't handle the strain. With a bigger, sturdier backhoe, the work progressed pretty quickly. All we hit was one boulder that wouldn't budge, so we dug around it, and that boulder is now part of our foundation.

Oh right, the concussion. That was a result of Art's not looking before he leaped. If he *had*, he'd have noticed the arm of the backhoe hanging there above the trench.

I was in the old, wrecked aqua-blue trailer, stripping paint off the windows we'd bought at a salvage yard, so I didn't see Art not look before he leaped. All Art remembered was leaping from one side of the trench and waking up *in* the trench.

What I *did* see was him coming toward me with blood dripping down his forehead.

"What happened to you?" I asked.

"I'm not sure," he said, a little vaguely.

I think jumping into the backhoe happened before he stepped on the nail ... or was it after? I know it was definitely before Greg and I dropped the beam on his head.

Whatever the order, I'm fairly convinced that before we started the project, Art made a pact with the devil. *This is a fairly dangerous undertaking,* he must have said, *so if things are going to happen to anybody, I want them to happen to **me**.* Which they did.

***

The footing pour went flawlessly. It had to. There was nowhere else for the cement to go except into the bottom of the trench. The truck poured, we prodded the cement to make sure there'd be no air pockets, and then as it began to set, we inserted re-bar or reinforcing bars, metal rods which would tie together the footing and the soon-to-be-poured walls.

By then, we'd come up with an idea for the rest of the foundation.

Knowing that we wanted to end up with foundation walls with rigid foam insulation on the outside to keep our floor as warm as possible, we decided to make minimal forms with rigid insulation already attached that would go atop the footing, then be backfilled, and remain there after the cement was poured. We made them from pressure treated wood, with sheets of rigid foam insulation attached to the outside, and used as little wood as possible, which made them somewhat less than rigid. But we used pieces of re-bar as spacers to keep the outside and inside from collapsing inward when we back-filled against their outer surfaces. In theory, the backfilled dirt would reinforce the forms so they couldn't blow out, and the cement itself would keep the forms from collapsing in. We knew that concrete had enormous pressure, but it would be completely contained, at least below ground.

The problem was the part of the foundation that had to be *above*-ground. About a foot of it. This was the part that was tricky. There wasn't going to be anything to support those forms except the forms themselves. And how were we going to build *those*?

After coming up with and discarding a bunch of ideas, we decided to use horizontal 2x12 boards as the aboveground forms. They would give us the correct height, and we could brace them with perpendicular 2x4s that would be attached, in turn, to stakes driven into the ground every eight feet or so. Voila. Well, at least in theory.

But before we get to that, let's fortify ourselves with our one early foundation success. The one we still gloat over.

For any of you who might have watched *This Old House* during the '90s, the use of foundation forms that went into the ground with insulation already applied and *stayed* in the ground had become an accepted method for building a foundation. But this

Fifty Acres, More or Less

was 1986. No one, as far as we knew, had thought of it yet. The *accepted* method was to dig a hugely oversized trench, pour a footing, place forms, pour the walls, remove the forms, apply insulation, and then backfill.

Because Pomfret had a population of only around 2500, word got around quickly that a professor from Boston was building his own house up on the hill, and for the most part, people were pleasant, helpful, and welcoming. Those were some of the reasons we decided to move to Pomfret in the first place. A few people, however, thought the whole thing was a hoot.

Someone in this latter group, who happened to have the same name as a famous dead poet … I'll call him Homer … would come up once in a while to see what we were up to and offer advice. He arrived one day when Art was in Cambridge and our unique foundation forms were almost completely installed. He was fascinated by them. He studied them, moving around the whole foundation, stroking his chin, scratching his head, squinting, making little noises. He looked at them from every angle. And then he started to laugh.

"Did you guys ever build a house before?"

Of course, it was a rhetorical question because he already knew the answer. He shook his head. "You can't do it like that. It ain't gonna work."

"Well, you might be right," I said. "And you might be wrong."

He left laughing. Maybe he's still laughing.

It reminded me of something that happened when I was a child. My father had always been a frustrated farmer, and when I was about six years old, he bought an old farm in New Hampshire. He didn't intend to farm, but to spend weekends and summers there, fixing it up, having a garden, enjoying the peace and quiet. Shortly after buying it, he decided to put in a pond across the road from the house and hired a local backhoe to come up on a Saturday morning to dig the hole. Word got around that the city people from Boston were digging a swimming hole, and shortly before the backhoe was due, a line of pick-ups arrived. They were local men who'd decided to watch the dig. They'd also come to watch the swimming hole fill up ... or more importantly, to watch it *not* fill up. I was just a kid, but I knew they were joking at my father's expense. "So, you think there's water down there?" "Gonna just bubble up like magic?" "Should'a brought my water wings." And then they'd chuckle.

My father chuckled right along with them, and I remember feeling angry that he wasn't setting them straight, that he was letting them make fun like that.

Anyway, the backhoe came, dug the hole, and the locals chatted and chuckled. I think my mother even served lemonade. Then, when the backhoe was finished and they pointed to the hole and said things like, "Hey, where's the water?" and "Looks a little damp over there to me," my father walked over to a spigot and turned it. Out gushed a stream of clear, cold spring water. Of course, he'd spent the month before laying plastic pipe from the spring up at the top of the hill. No pump was necessary. Gravity did it all. The men went silent. This time it was my father who chuckled. Then they all went home. Even during summer droughts that swimming hole had a constant supply of water that was still pouring in forty years later.

In Pomfret, Homer's misgivings must have got around, because a few days later, the owner of the concrete company we'd called to do the pour showed up. He was a little more thoughtful than Homer had been. He squatted down and studied it for a while, then he nodded. "That's a good idea. That's a really good idea. It should work fine."

And it did. Well, almost.

You have to understand that there was a lot of work going on simultaneously. We hardly ever worked on one thing exclusively, because there were too many other things pulling on our time.

Fifty Acres, More or Less

The utility trench was still in-process, we'd had to dig the trench between the well and the house and install the well pipe through the foundation, excavate for the septic tank, and while all this was going on, we were also out scavenging wrecking yards for windows, doors, lumber, anything that would cut costs.

Because we had our fingers in too many pies, we were building the forms for the above-ground portion of the foundation the evening before the cement truck was to come. Plus we'd had to spend time pumping water out of the foundation trench because, of course, it had just rained, and now the cement truck was coming first thing in the morning.

We'd been at it non-stop since April, five long months, and every board we'd cut for the forms had to be cut by hand because there was still no electricity. It was late, getting dark, and when we finally finished the top-most forms, Art looked at the supporting structure that was supposed to hold the 2x12s in place.

"It's not strong enough," he said.

I hated it when he sounded that way. Totally calm, but absolutely dire at the same time.

"What do you mean?" I asked. "What's not strong enough??"

He pointed. "The supports. We don't have enough 2x4s supporting the 2x12s."

"But this is how we planned it," I said. "How can you suddenly decide it's not right?"

"Because on paper it seemed sufficient," he said, "but now I can see it's not. The whole thing could blow out. We need more supports."

It was getting dark. We searched. But we'd only bought what we thought we'd need. We had no extra 2x4s. And the lumber yards had closed hours ago.

"We need to call off the pour," Art said. "I'll get up early and go down and call them. We can be ready again in three days."

Tima Smith

For me, at that point, losing a day felt like losing a year. We were supposed to have the whole house framed already. We were supposed to have a roof on. But September was around the corner and we didn't even have the hint of a wall up.

"We have a support every eight feet," I said. "That's plenty. It's only twelve inches of concrete, and I don't want to wait another three days. I'm so sick of this foundation! They're fine. The forms are fine!"

And maybe because he was tired, too, and just as anxious as I to keep things moving, he acquiesced.

***

The cement truck driver was the same man who had poured the footing. He'd been more than helpful then, doing the pour slowly and even getting out of the truck to help us move the cement. This time, if he had any doubts about the structure supporting the 2x12 forms, he didn't say anything. He just began the pour, very slowly, while we ran around pushing poles into the cement to prevent air pockets and to move the concrete along.

There's something about having a gigantic cement mixer pumping concrete into a finite space that makes your blood pressure rise. For one thing, concrete weighs approximately 150 pounds per cubic foot. It's heavy, nasty stuff. To give you an example, a basketball filled with concrete would weigh over a hundred pounds. Mixes can vary from too dry to too wet. But you have to have a lot of experience to judge that. We simply had to trust that this mix was right. One thing we did know was that cement sets in its own time, not yours. And we'd heard all the horror stories. About the man who waded into the concrete barefoot to push it around and burned off all the skin on his feet and legs. About the forms that burst and filled someone's entire basement with two feet of concrete. These were the things on our minds as we pushed and prodded the stuff and watched it rise.

Fifty Acres, More or Less

Of course, the below-ground forms filled no-problem. Then the concrete reached the top forms, and within minutes, to our horror, the 2x12s began to bulge.

It lives in my memory as one of those moments when you can't quite believe what's happening, when you know that everything you can do probably won't be enough, and most especially when you wish you could go back in time and do things differently.

At first, all Art and I could think to do was try to hold the boards in place against the push of the concrete with our bare hands. But then the driver stopped the flow, jumped down, and began jamming anything he could find against the supports to keep them from blowing out completely — cinder blocks, rocks, a wheelbarrow, eventually, his foot.

We stared at the boards. Had they stopped bulging or was it just our imagination? "I think they're stable," the driver said. Then we all ran around and dragged back anything that could act as weight to hold those boards in place ... a couple of car tires, jugs of water, the boxes that held our still-packed table and circular saws.

It was a desperate situation, and at that point we had no choice but to continue. The driver started the pour again, but very very slowly this time. I bet we didn't even breathe. And by some miracle, the forms stopped bulging and held until they were filled.

Oh, they had widened in a few places, but they didn't blow out. And we all just looked at one another, knowing exactly how lucky we'd been. How close we'd come to spewing cement all over the place, breaking apart our forms, ruining our foundation. And I think the driver was just as happy as we were. Glad for us. Glad to have helped.

When he left, when I listened to the sound of his cement truck receding down the hill, I felt the biggest sense of relief I'd had in my building life to that point. In fact, I can still feel it.

Tima Smith

Of course I acknowledged the fact that Art had been very right and I had been very wrong. And he didn't do what I might have, didn't even get close to an I-told-you-so look on his face.

"Just another war story," he said. "We'll need plenty of those when this is all over and we have nothing else to do but talk about it."

That night, we celebrated at the local Burger King salad bar. No more cement trucks! No more forms! No more puddling! No more leveling and screeding and racing to do it all before the concrete set for eternity!

***

Normally, there would have been one more pour, the slab for the floor. But we'd decided to pass on any more concrete adventures. We chose to do the floor our own way, and pretty much for free, with a combination of stone from our land and brick. Eventually, when we had time, we'd lay down a layer of plastic to keep moisture out, then a layer of the same rigid foam insulation we'd attached to the perimeter of the underground foundation. After that, we'd lay areas of brick in the kitchen, bathroom, and living room, and stone in the through-hallway, all set in a dry mix of cement and sand. We wanted a floor that would act as a heat sink for solar gain, and we wanted something a bit classier than concrete.

It would be a labor-intensive floor. A floor we wouldn't get to until the house was framed and the roof was on. What we didn't know at the time was that we'd be walking around on dirt a lot longer than we could ever imagine.

Fifty Acres, More or Less

II

Fourteen. That's how old I was when I started dating my first husband. Fourteen. I kept stuffed animals on my bed. There were posters on my wall of Fabian and Paul Anka and Pat Boone. I listened to Elvis, but he wasn't my favorite.

I thought I was very grown up, but I was just a child. Lots of the girls I went to junior high with had boyfriends. I sort of wanted one, too, although I had no idea what I'd do with one. I didn't particularly like boys. They often acted like idiots. But then a boy asked me out. I wasn't even sure I wanted to go out. What did you do? How did you talk to someone you didn't even know? But everyone else was doing it. It was like a rite of passage.

And no one told me I could put it off. That it might be better to put it off.

So I went out on my first date. Nervous. Not all that happy about it. But it wasn't a disaster, just mostly awkward and strange. And for some reason I could never figure out, he asked me out again. And then again.

Having a boyfriend meant the phone rang regularly. It meant a guaranteed date on weekends and for every dance. It defined me at a time when I had no idea who I was or would one day be. I was, if nothing else, somebody's girlfriend.

And there was always one nagging question ... what if no one else ever wanted me to be his girlfriend? What if this was my one chance. There were boys I liked more, but they didn't seem to know I existed. And there were a few boys I liked who liked me back, boys who were funny or interesting or smart, but none of them looked even a little bit like Frankie Avalon or Pat Boone. They didn't seem to equate with 'boyfriend.' I remember one who was so funny, so nice, so smart that I'll probably always remember him. He asked me to his

Tima Smith

senior prom. But I had a 'boyfriend' so I didn't go with him. I wish I had.

After a year or so, I got bored with the boyfriend I had and broke it off. But it was as if I'd been tattooed or marked in some indelible way as someone's 'girlfriend.' The fact that he lived in a different town and went to a different high school made a difference. The grapevine didn't travel that far. And exactly what I feared most of all happened. The phone didn't ring. I stayed home for eight weekends in a row. I got scared. And when he called me, again, I gave in. I was almost sixteen, heading toward old maid-hood. Why, I should have been wondering, did I have to be 'liked' by a boy? Any boy? Why wasn't it enough just to like myself?? And two years later, with a year of college under my belt and a newly growing confidence that there were, after all, other boys out there who would like me, I got pregnant.

CHAPTER EIGHT

Near-Death Experiences – and Less Serious Injuries

To keep us from getting too giddy early on, we had a disaster. Not the kind of disaster that calls for an ambulance or a blood transfusion, but enough of a disaster just the same.

Our friend Jerry was up from the Cape for the weekend. Greg was there, and my Michael and his friend Steve. We were taking a mid-afternoon break, sitting around talking, all of us except Steve, who was doing some clearing with the Case on the slope where the utility trench cut up from the driveway through the woods to the top of the hill.

I was sitting with a view in that direction when Steve appeared. He was walking slowly, and there was something in the way he was carrying himself — in the way he was moving, that set off an alarm in my head. I got up and started toward him, and as soon as I was close enough to see the look on his face, I knew something was very wrong.

"What happened?" I asked.

His face was the color of putty, his voice croaked. "I had an accident." He swallowed. "The dozer turned over."

It was a potential, along with major limb mutilations, that had given me anxiety attacks from the second Art first drove the Case up the hill. It was a damn heavy piece of machinery, low and wide, and it looked impossible to tip over, but with something heavy in its bucket, or on a slope, you had to pay constant attention to your center of gravity. Art had come close to tipping it forward or backward moving heavy boulders. But with a forward or backward tip you could always control it by being quick on the bucket controls. Lowering the bucket fast always brought it back level. But on a slope, there was the potential for a sideways tip, and a sideways tip was something else. Once you were on the edges of those tracks, nothing you did with the controls was going to have any effect.

Steve might have been a freshman in college, but he was looking more like an eight-year-old at the moment. I grabbed his arms. "My God, Steve," I said, "are you okay?"

He nodded. "I jumped."

He *was* okay, although it took a while for his color to return. The Case was another story.

It lay on its side, tracks pointing downhill, on the steepest part of the incline, and we all stood there staring at it.

The main consensus was that Steve was lucky. Lucky to be quick and agile and okay. Then came the big question: how the heck were we going to get this thing back on its feet?

It weighed somewhere in the vicinity of three tons and it was on an eight-degree slope. To right it by rolling it *up* the slope, we'd have to turn it around so that the tracks were facing uphill. But we had no equipment powerful enough to do that or powerful enough to roll it over on the uphill once it was in position. Rolling it downhill back onto its tracks would be easier. We could probably use its own weight to overcome inertia. But how did you start *that* process? And more importantly, how did you control it once it started? How were we supposed to keep it from continuing downhill … another hundred feet down to the driveway? It didn't look terrifically damaged, and we wanted to keep it that way.

Once the initial reactions of relief and despair passed, everyone moved on to figuring out a solution.

Mine was simple, but costly. Hire a bigger machine.

The only solution that wasn't going to cost an arm and a leg was to do it ourselves, and that's the one everyone else favored.

"We have two come-a-longs," Art said. "If we attach them on the downhill side between the tractor and two trees, and tie off the uphill side with…"

I couldn't listen any more. It seemed just plain crazy. But all the guys seemed to agree that was the way to handle it.

"Do you have any idea," I said, "how dangerous this could be?" But I might as well have been making no sound at all.

I followed Art and Greg and Michael to the storage shed, where they dragged out a coil of chain and two coils of rope.

"Are you sure these are strong enough?" I asked.

Greg looked at the rope. It was half-inch nylon line, the kind you'd use for tying up a 30' sailboat to a dock. He nodded. "Sure. It's fine."

I eyed the chain, which was long, but not very thick.

"Don't worry about it, Mum," Greg said. "It'll work."

Michael, who'd been born with a more highly-developed caution gene, gave me a look and shrugged. Then they hoisted the chain between them and headed for the Case.

Art seemed to be the only one who sensed that my worry was edging toward panic. He put his arm around me. "I wouldn't try it if I thought it was too dangerous," he said. "It'll be okay."

But all I could see was the Case crashing straight on down the hill, ending up a heap of useless twisted steel. And granted, I didn't much like that machine, but we needed it.

"What if we end up putting it permanently out of commission just to save some money?" I asked.

"I don't think that will happen," he said, picking up the come-alongs.

"Why don't we at least make some calls?" I followed him across the yard. "Just to find out how much someone would charge to come in with a ... with a..." I didn't know what would have to come in.

"A crane?" Art said. "A whole lot."

***

On the side of the hill, they all got busy hatching the plan. And as I listened and watched, it began to dawn on me that the Case crashing down the hill was the least worst thing that could happen. Three tons of steel had the potential of snapping anything trying to hold it. What if *that* happened? Even a nylon rope breaking under that kind of stress would snap back like a bullet. Steve had already come way too close to being hurt or worse, and now there were four other people about to do something just as dangerous.

But by then, what had started out as a dismal prospect had morphed into a sense of grim determination tinged with a palpable edge of adventure. At least for everyone but me. And I knew that nothing I said was going make one bit of difference.

By the time everything was attached and places were assigned, it was getting dark. So the adventure was postponed until the next morning. Well now, I thought, how perfect. One whole night to lie awake and think of all the things that could go horribly, terribly wrong.

***

The next day Steve begged off. He'd had enough the day before and couldn't even watch. I didn't want to watch either, but I figured there needed to be someone there who could run for help.

The come-alongs looked pitifully puny for the job, which they were. And I know that the fact they might explode under stress half-way through the process was on everyone's mind because they all admitted it. At least, once it was all over they did.

Art and Jerry were the come-along pumpers. They had to stand right over the handles and crank, and if the come-alongs self-destructed, they were the ones who stood the most chance of losing some vital part of their anatomies.

Fifty Acres, More or Less

"What if they tear apart?" I asked. "Someone could get his head taken off!"

But I might as well have been howling at a big empty sky.

The chain and two ropes were tied to big trees on the high side, leaving just enough slack, they hoped, to let the Case roll onto its tracks, but no farther. I urged Michael and Greg, who were to mark progress from different angles, to scope out trees to hide behind when the tie-offs were under the most stress.

I positioned myself close enough to see everything and far enough away so no one would hear me praying. I couldn't stand still so I paced back and forth, hoping they'd see the folly of it all but knowing they wouldn't.

Art and Jerry started cranking, the come-alongs went taut, and the Case started to move. Up, up, up it inched.

"I think this one's distorting," Jerry yelled, his eyes glued on his come-along. "If I yell again, everyone hit the ground."

They cranked some more. The high side tie-offs rose in the air, the Case rose, too, more and more, until finally it teetered on the edge of one track, and then, with a few more cranks, thundered down onto both.

Then the uphill track left the ground and the machine started to tip over again. That's when my heart stopped. Everyone yelled. Art and Jerry, who were fifteen or twenty feet away and directly in its path, ran in opposite directions. Michael and Greg each dove behind a tree. The ropes and the chain on the high side strained, and then one rope snapped.

I still remember the sound of that rope breaking, a high metallic crack.

The Case, atilt on one track, stood absolutely still for one second before it settled back onto both, the chain and one rope still holding. It was right side up again.

Tima Smith

Art, Michael, Jerry, Greg — they all reappeared intact. Then they gave a cheer, and I noticed my heart had started beating again.

The after-game replays went on for an entire evening.

"Christ, take a look at the way this chain dug into the tree!"

"I saw that thing start to go over and all I could think was, "'Holy shit!'"

"Did you hear that rope crack when it snapped? I swear it flew three inches over my head!"

"She didn't come up half as hard as I thought she would."

"I suppose you know those come-alongs were rated for about a tenth that weight?"

"Yeah, I kept expecting them to blow into a million pieces before the thing was even off the ground."

And I? I realized I'd suddenly developed a terrific headache.

***

The come-alongs were too distorted to ever use again so we threw them away. The Case, which had suffered more damage than it showed, was repaired at a cost of $1500.00. And the success of the righting? Well, it still hasn't convinced me that it was worth the risk. But Art was right. It's a terrific story.

***

Once the actual building started, there was a lot of debris around the building site. We should have been neater, but all our attention was on the process of *making* the mess. Cleaning it up wasn't part of the menu.

Which is probably why Art stepped on the nail. It was sticking up out of a board that was lying on the ground, and it was long enough to go right through the sole of his boot and up into the ball of his foot. He had to pull it out with a hammer.

"Have you had a tetanus shot?" I asked, looking at the ragged puncture.

"Sure," he said. "About twenty-five years ago."

He went to the emergency room for the shot, and ended up wishing he'd stayed home.

"They had to go all the way up inside," he told me later, wincing just talking about it. "They said that was very important, to clean it out properly. It felt like they were using a drill bit with pointed teeth."

He limped for a few days. And although we didn't become neatniks or even bother to start pulling or even banging the pointed end flat, we at least turned over every board with a nail in it so that the head was up and the dangerous end went into the ground.

***

Ladders presented a particular threat that had nothing to do with height. It took a few konks on the head and some fiery accusations before we got into the habit of *never leaving tools on the top of the ladder.*

Say I was working on the ladder with a hammer, then I came down to get another tool. I'd leave the hammer on the ladder. Then Art would need the ladder, move it, and get konked when the hammer fell off. He'd be irate for a few minutes. "How could you do anything so stupid?" he'd say, rubbing his head or his shoulder or his knee. Then later that afternoon he'd do the exact same thing to me.

***

We'd been told before we started building that one thing we'd need was a good chiropractor. "You're going to throw your backs out all over the place, and a chiropractor can save you a lot of lost work days," another self-builder told us.

It seemed a reasonable potential, but we never had that particular problem. And we never got sick. Which probably means that living outdoors is better for you than you might think.

Tima Smith

***

Amazingly, the only other potentially deadly thing that happened was after the first floor walls were framed and we were working on the ceiling stringers. We needed hefty stringers (8x12s) to hold up the second floor, and, besides, we wanted hefty stringers because we liked the way they looked. But we couldn't afford to buy actual beams, so we manufactured our own by nailing together four 2x12s. Lengthwise, the 36' house was divided into three sections by four beams that ran front to back, one on the top of each end wall and two centered between them twelve feet apart. These beams (and the entire second floor) extended two feet beyond the first-floor front (or south) wall. This extension provided an overhang to act as a sunshade in the summer when the sun was high, but would allow full sunshine in the winter, when the sun's angle was low. The hefty stringers were notched into these beams perpendicularly at four-foot intervals.

One day, Greg and Art and I were going up ladders putting these hefty stringers in place and nailing. It was Art's turn to take a rest, and he was standing there watching Greg and me when one of us (neither of us can remember who, which shows how convenient a thing memory can be) dropped his/her end. Right on top of Art. It hit him on the head, and it must have been a glancing blow, had to be, because although it staggered him, he didn't go down and he didn't go out.

Greg and I froze for one horrible second, but there was no blood, no crumpled form twitching on the floor, just Art's knees almost going out from under him. I still don't understand how something that heavy could have caused so little damage. Although it could have had something to do with the hardness of the thing it fell on.

***

Of course there were the usual injuries you'd expect … smashed thumbs and fingers, black and blue shins, splinters. Greg twisted his ankle jumping off the second floor and turned green enough to make us think it must be broken. Which it wasn't. But it was a bad sprain and he limped for a long time.

Then there were close calls that caught you in the stomach whenever you thought of what *could* have happened. The time Art was cutting firewood with a chain saw and came so close to his leg that the chain tore through his jeans but didn't touch his skin.

And there was the weekend Brian brought some reinforcement from college to help frame the second floor. He and his friend Pat Cloney were banging together a wall section, Brian nailing studs at the top of the wall and Pat nailing at the bottom. They got a little too close to each other at one point, and the claw on Pat's hammer caught Brian on the bridge of his nose right between his eyes. Brian had two small incisions where the points of the claw just broke the skin. Sometimes, maybe most of the time, you just get lucky.

Tima Smith

III

At the age of eighteen, my actual 'growing up' was replaced with simply acquiring grown-up things. A wedding ring. An apartment to keep clean. Then diapers. I spent my wedding night crying. I couldn't stop. Did part of me know something I couldn't consciously understand?

I ended up caught between two worlds. In one, many of the girls I'd grown up with went to a two-year secretary school and then into office run by men, where they might meet their future husband. Some girls went off for four years to become nurses or teachers, but most had already chosen their future husband and were smart enough to know they'd have to work, at least for a while. Teaching was ideal because it gave summers off to care for future children.

I had some vague idea about studying psychology. Maybe I wanted to understand the whys of my decisions. Although they didn't seem like decisions. Just things that happened.

The girls just a few years behind me were the girls who threw away their bras and went to Woodstock. Birth control changed everything. It just didn't work for me. Instead, it made me half-crazy. They wouldn't find out for a decade that there was an excessive dose of hormones in those early pills. Five kids. Four in diapers at the same time. A husband who simply wouldn't grow up or take responsibility or even help just a little. My kids were everything. The outside world spun by, and I only suspected I was in trouble when someone asked me how old I was and I said, "eighteen." I was really twenty-five.

CHAPTER NINE

Two One-Track Minds

The summer went by in a whirl of learning how to do *everything.* When we weren't working harder than we'd ever worked in our lives, we were planning, making decisions, making mistakes, inching ahead. Sometimes we were frustrated, but most of the time we were okay. We had this beautiful piece of land; we were living closer to nature than we ever had; and somehow we were managing to actually learn the skills we needed to get the job done. Essentially, it was satisfying.

It was just taking way too long.

And it was all-consuming.

There was no time to read a paper or listen to the radio. And of course there was no TV. Aside from the house, which people were either genuinely interested in or just polite about, we had absolutely nothing else to talk about. Not that we saw many people. We couldn't cook; we were living in a tent; we were usually preoccupied with things no one else cared one whit about. The best friends we had were the guys at the lumber yard, who were great, by the way ... Dave and Ed and Alan and Gary and Fred. They not only provided the materials we needed, they provided conversation. We knew all about Dave's Harley and Ed's kids and Alan's new baby girl. Fred, who was a fine carpenter, gave us mini-lessons on anything we asked about. He prevented us from doing all sorts of things the wrong way, and he always did it with grace and a sincere desire to help.

People did come by to visit now and then, curious about what on earth we were doing, but usually it felt like an interruption we couldn't afford. And the only good thing about living in a tent is that when people do come to visit, they don't stay long.

Tima Smith

Food was something we stopped for only when we were blind from hunger or it got too dark to do any work. We tried cooking out on a grill for a while, but grills seem essentially designed for meat. Our vegetarian tofu either burst into flames or broke up and fell down into the coals. And besides, cooking took too much time. Mainly we lived on granola bars. *Kudos*. I still can't even stand the sight of them on the supermarket shelf.

Occasionally we ate at a local restaurant that served adequate, cheap food and had the greatest pecan pie I've ever tasted. But mostly, we drove an extra ten minutes to Burger King because it was cheaper. We showed up at their salad bar so much, the people who worked there began to notice when we *didn't* come in. "Hey," they'd say, "what happened last night? You didn't come in!"

***

By the time we began framing the house in mid-September, Michael and Steve had gone back to school in Washington. Brian was in college in central Massachusetts and Greg had taken a job about an hour away from Brian. Lauren had started her senior year of high school, and between an after-school job and sports, she was only there in the evening. So Art and I were alone, except on weekends when Greg would show up by himself or with a friend, or Michael E drove down from Vermont to see how we were doing and lend a hand.

At that point, we were at least three months behind. But there was nothing to do except keep moving ahead. We had electricity by then, a single plug and extension cords, and a phone. And that made it feel almost like Versailles.

After three months of preparation, we'd watched the utilities be installed in one day. A worker from the telephone company had literally tossed the telephone wire into the trench in less than an hour. The electric company, on the other hand, had come with a crew and equipment and a serious, careful attitude about their cable, which had to lay right and uncoil properly.

Fifty Acres, More or Less

They arrived early in the morning, installed a transformer about 150 feet from the house and began to lay the cable in the trench from the transformer, down the slope, past the site of the great Case tip-over, and then down to the driveway. It was a slow installation. It took all day.

Then, late in the afternoon, they discovered they had about three hundred feet to go to the street, but not quite three hundred feet of cable left on the spool. These careful people, who demanded only the finest bed of sand for their cable without so much as a pebble to be seen, decided to stretch the cable in order to avoid an extra splice. In fact, they stretched it so tight that the cable wasn't even lying in the bottom of the trench.

"Are you sure it's okay to have it suspended like that?" we asked, "and stretched that tight? What about the sand it's supposed to be lying on? How can we cover it with sand when it's a foot in the air?" But it was the end of a long day, and the street connection was in sight, and all of a sudden the fuss over doing it 'just so' seemed to disappear.

We took pictures, just in case.

Both the phone cable and the electric cable are still doing their jobs almost twenty years later, although ten to twelve years is generally about as long as they last before needing repair. We're told the electric cable usually fails in the winter, when the ground is freezing and thawing. There's a device that pinpoints the problem so the entire length of cable doesn't have to be unearthed, and because the electric company *did* end up guaranteeing it, they will pay for the dig and the repair. But every time we lose our electricity we wonder if that delicate cable that couldn't withstand the friction of *one* pebble has finally been breached.

Once we had electricity, we could have a pressure tank installed and hooked up to the well pump. Running water! The pressure tank looked like a fat bright blue hot water heater, and it was the only vertical thing inside the foundation. It talked to the

Tima Smith

well pump whenever it needed water, the well pump filled it up, and all we had to do was turn a spigot. Running water ... it was miraculous.

Electricity, a phone, water. We walked around in a constant state of amazement.

At that point, the temporary breaker box and the pressure tank were the only things we hadn't put in ourselves, and it was a novelty to have someone working there who didn't have to take time out to look something up in a book.

Fifty Acres, More or Less

IV

To try and find a self other than 'wife & mother' I audited college courses. No money for actual tuition. And I read. Two books in each bathroom — that was the only time I could be alone, with the kids talking at me through the door. I didn't mind. I loved them more than anything in the world. It had always been me and them. As though they barely had a father. Or didn't want the one they had. He was nobody's person of choice, and that bothered me, but it didn't seem to bother him a bit.

Maybe, I realize now, he'd never wanted any of it. So he accepted as little as he could get away with. And to make sure he could get away with accepting as little as possible, he wore anger like a sword. It was always ready. So if you were a smart wife, you went along. And if you were a smart kid, you stayed out of his way. But despite his bullying, he was actually totally dependent on me. I just didn't figure that out for a very long time. I was the one holding our illusionary world together. His whole life was dependent on me. We all believed he was the one with the power, but it was really mine all that time. I just didn't know it. And if I had, I wouldn't have known how to use it. It was easier to play the roles rather than examine them. The handsome, happy young family. The smart beautiful kids. The happy marriage. Not that the illusion was easy to live. I remember walking the house when I was alone, thinking 'I can't do this anymore. I can't do this for the rest of my life.' But I kept doing it anyway. I did it for seventeen years...

Tima Smith

CHAPTER TEN

Second Hand Stuff

For thirty-five years, I hadn't even known wrecking and salvage yards existed. But I ended up spending a lot of time walking through one in Springfield, Massachusetts and another in Stamford, Connecticut. Salvage yards are places where pieces of houses end up. And although they've changed in the intervening years, having become more upscale and expensive, in the late '80s, they were a gold mine.

They were huge places with most things in the open air, and you could find just about anything you needed among acres of exterior doors, windows, toilets, sinks, and lumber. Inside, there was lighting, hardware, interior doors, flooring, and things you can't even begin to imagine a use for. Everything was cheap. A lot of it should have been free. But if you picked through carefully, you could find real gems.

You can't really go to these places with a shopping list. You have to be flexible. And you have to be willing to use your imagination. It's a little like cooking without a recipe. You won't know what you're going to end up with until you sit down to eat, but luckily our tastes were just enough off the edge of normal to make buying used possible.

We needed to know the dimensions of doors and windows before we could frame the first floor, so visits to wrecking yards became an important part of the soup that first summer.

Our house plan called for a first floor that was essentially free of interior walls. That meant a combination construction. Normal stud construction for the exterior walls, and post and beam construction to hold the house up everywhere else. We'd decided on higher than normal ceilings for the first floor, nine feet. Most ceilings are seven, but I'd lived for fifteen years in a high-ceilinged Victorian, which I liked. Art had lived for fifteen years in a bungalow where you could touch the ceilings by merely raising your hand, so he was tired of low-ceiling claustrophobia.

It's one of the perks of building your own house, exercising personal preference even if your preferences aren't always reasoned or logical.

As far as our high ceiling went, there was one thing we didn't give much thought to: the fact that heat rises. It never occurred to us that on future freezing winter nights, the only truly warm place in the house would be four feet above our heads.

More or less in the center of the first floor would be the stairs, and we planned to have a 6x6 post at each corner of the stairway, which would support the 6x6 posts directly above them, and then, in turn, the ceiling beams, which, of course, would support the roof.

During our first trip to a salvage yard, we found a pile of pine posts that might once have been part of a playground. They weren't 6x6, they were 12x12. Two of them were notched in an interesting way at the top, reminiscent of a totem pole. They were a fraction of the cost of lumber-yard posts, plus they were the right length. We thought they were interesting, so we bought four of them.

They were enormously heavy, but somehow we got them into the back of our pick-up, and somehow the truck's suspension held up for the ride home. Although we had to drive with the tailgate down to accommodate their length, they were so heavy they didn't even slide out while we were driving up our hill.

We ended up using the two notched posts at either end of one side of the stairway, notches facing into the living room. They're quite impressive, and no one has ever come into the house and *not* asked about them.

Tima Smith

We wanted lots of windows, especially on the south facing wall of the first floor, and discovered why small, inexpensive houses have few windows and large expensive houses have many. Windows can eat up a good third of your budget, and although we were determined to have passive solar heat, we didn't have fifteen thousand dollars to spend on windows. So instead we spent fifteen hundred.

At the Stamford, Connecticut salvage yard, where there were easily five hundred used windows, a particular group of windows caught our eye. I can't say why, exactly, but even from a distance they stood out from the rest. They were wooden casements that opened in, instead of out the way most do. They had wooden storm attachments and attractive brass hardware, and when we asked a passing employee how much they were, he squinted at them for a second and said, "Five bucks a window?"

We bought all of them. Eight windows. Forty dollars. They would be the second floor windows for the bedrooms, with one left over for the kitchen.

In between digging the utility trench and working on the foundation, I probably put in thirty hours removing coats and coats of paint from each one of those windows. It was boring and messy and slow, and I always ended up thinking we'd made a bad bargain. At least until I got down to the bare wood and saw the name stamped on each edge. Anderson. Old-style Anderson casements, as elegant and weather-tight as the day they were made.

Although the second-floor window problem got solved fairly early, we still needed a large amount of glass for the solar gain on the first floor, and we weren't having any luck there at all. There were always a few windows for sale here and there, but not the number we needed … eight or ten sliding glass doors for that south facing wall in the living room.

We were at the point of giving up on the passive solar plan, drastically cutting the number of windows and buying new, when Art happened to see an ad in a local paper. A business in nearby

Fifty Acres, More or Less

Rhode Island was selling a trailer load of sliding glass doors they'd removed from an office building in Cambridge, Mass. Each door measured seven feet high by five feet wide. The glass was tempered and insulated. And the price was twenty dollars per door.

By dismantling each door, we ended up with two windows, and bought enough to give us a thirty-two foot wall of glass across the front of the living room, plus several extras for use elsewhere.

It was a good thing we had them, too, the extras, because after we removed the sliding door frame, there was still a narrow metal frame around each piece of glass that needed to be removed as well. The only way to remove this strip was with a hammer.

"Don't bang so hard," I warned Art.

"I'm not banging hard," he said, whacking away, "it only *looks* like I am." Whack whack whack.

"No," I said, it looks like you're banging hard because you *are*. Can't you just tap it?"

He gave me a look that said, *I'm doing this so just let me do it, okay?*'

By then we'd become good at reading a situation and judging just how far we could push each other before a hammer flew or things got said that needed to be apologized for later. We were both slow to reach the boiling point, which helped, but suggestions about doing things differently (read *my* way) tended to make each of us defensive. We got better at collaborating and handling criticism and accepting offers of alternate ways of doing things, but early on, a suggestion to 'hold the saw *straight* for Pete's sake' or 'I said *push*, not *pull*!' or asking a simple question like 'didn't you *measure* it before you cut it?' or 'where in hell did you put the T-square *now*??' was taken personally. Very *very* personally.

Anyway, because I sensed a certain tenseness in Art, I shut up and watched him whack until there was a new sound, one that made him stop his hammer in mid-air.

Tima Smith

It's amazing how many beads there are to sweep up after fifteen square feet of tempered glass shatters. The process, though, as the initial crack spreads throughout the entire window in a kind of expanding spider web, and the noise it makes right through to the explosion of beads is pretty spectacular.

We lost three windows this way. And not all of them were Art's fault.

The only windows we bought new were two roof windows and two small Anderson casements, one for each bathroom. To add cross ventilation in the living room, we paid less than retail for two over-sized Anderson casements which a customer had ordered, but never picked up from our local lumber yard.

Most of our lighting fixtures, inside and outside, came from salvage yards, and the hardwood paneled doors throughout the second floor came free from a house that was being remodeled. The wood paneling on many of our walls came free from a neighboring lumber mill, 1/2"x2"x16' strips, clear pine trimmings the mill had no use for. And yes, it was labor intensive since each piece only covered a two-inch width. But it was absolutely free! And we thought the subtle shadings that made it unusable by the lumber yard created an interesting wall.

For one small wall on the first floor and another on the second, we ended up dismantling twelve-foot wooden shipping containers from Germany, which we bought for six dollars a box. Unplaned, they have a decidedly rustic look, and I'm not particularly crazy about them, especially when my arm brushes the wall and I get fifteen splinters all at once. These walls are on my own personal re-do list. And some day, we'll take them down and put up something more derma-friendly.

Then there are the big oak Victorian exterior double doors Art salvaged from the house he'd lived in, the fifteen-dollar antique pedestal sink from a salvage yard, all the second-hand appliances ... a refrigerator, a double oven, an electric cook top ... all of which were still working ten years later.

Fifty Acres, More or Less

V

The boat. We took up sailing. The idea of it was wonderful; the actuality, not so much. I read that some personalities take on the personae of 'overbearing captain' and turn into Ahab on the water. It's true. Of course, there were lovely moments ... the sea, the sky, the peace, the quiet ... but I suffered from chronic nausea unless I was constantly on deck, and my ex continued to suffer from chronic Ahabness.

It didn't make for quality weekends. We didn't have the money we needed for a boat that would comfortably accommodate seven people, but it was the only thing we did as a family, and that was important. Then my ex had an idea. Let's build a boat. Maybe, he said, we'd do it ourselves. A family project. I was such a sucker for anything we could do as a family.

I envisioned building it in the backyard. Something we could all be involved in. The kids would learn from it. Maybe it would even create a better relationship between them and their father. And since he tended to get completely over-involved in everything he did, it was something that would keep him very busy and in the backyard.

But then the plan morphed into something unrecognizable. Suddenly, it wasn't going to be a boat to sail on weekends. It was going to be a boat to live on. To sail around the world on! All of us? I said. Yes, all of us. A really big boat, he said. Fifty feet. And steel would be best. In the backyard? I asked. No, of course not. In Canada. There was a company there. How were we going to pay for that? I said. We'd re-mortgage the house. He'd already made the decision.

And who knew, maybe it would work. Maybe everything would be okay once the boat was built. We'd all be okay. Happy. A family. Off on a great adventure. Besides, it was easier to let him run with it. I

Tima Smith

had five kids to take care of. I was trying to learn to write. Helping run our photography business. And how was this crazy thing ever going to actually happen, anyway? It would run its course the way everything else had. It was an impossible idea. Too big. Too expensive. Too crazy.

But it was his boat, his plan, and it took him over, while we all just sat there and watched, taking slow steps away from the whole thing for an entire year. Waiting for it to implode. And implode it did, but not in the way I expected. The boat builder went bankrupt, and it was going to take every penny we had to make the final payment still due. But even then, the boat would remain locked up inside the bankrupt boat building until the complications of the bankruptcy were straightened out and the boat could be released.

The kids and I took a deep breath. Fate seemed to have intervened and put an end to the craziness. It would take a long time for the bankruptcy to unfold, and then we'd get our money back. We'd put that, along with the re-finance money we still had in the bank, into the mortgage. Sanity would reign.

CHAPTER ELEVEN

VISITORS

Although family and friends were curious or interested or just plain unbelieving about what we were doing, we didn't have a lot of company. For one thing, there was nowhere to entertain people — no comfortable place to sit, no place to prepare food. And we were so constantly busy and under such time pressure that stopping for several hours of socializing wasn't something we were particularly anxious to do very often.

Occasionally though, someone would express such interest in seeing what was going on that we'd find ourselves with visitors. Although at this point there wasn't much to see because practically everything we'd done was buried deep underground.

If our guests had any experience with building or carpentry, they asked lots of questions and hung on our answers, which was hugely encouraging. But if a visitor had no familiarity with all those systems we'd been working on for five months, what we had to show turned out to be about as interesting as dirt for them and hugely discouraging for us.

"This is the foundation," we'd say, pointing to the one-foot-high cement wall sticking up above ground.

"Ohhh," someone might say, looking at it with a lot more interest than it deserved. Or, "Wow." Or, "Very nice."

One person, Benjamin, an old friend of Art's who seemed to be elsewhere when they were handing out the capacity for tact and who had already told Art he should have his head examined for 'going off on this stupid tangent' (which, of course, included me) walked the entire perimeter of the foundation, stopping

Tima Smith

occasionally, and finally asked, "Why is it so wide in some places and narrow in others?"

No one else had seemed to notice that yet.

"Well," Art said, obviously reluctant to get into it, "the forms spread a bit during the pour." He cleared his throat. "But once the walls go up, it will all look uniform. It was just the interior boards that buckled."

The friend looked at Art, then back at the foundation. He didn't say anything, just shook his head, as in ... *what a damn shame that you've come to <u>this</u>*.

***

One day Art got a letter from someone out of his past. Now, you have to understand that Art *did* have a past. He'd been a bachelor for more than twenty years, and with the letters and photos and bits of memorabilia that surfaced in our packing and moving, sometimes I wondered how he'd had time in those twenty years for anything else.

Some of these 'people he'd known' were rather recent, and I have to admit I was jealous. Before we'd left Massachusetts, at least three had left warm phone messages, one had left a hot little note on his door, and one other had dropped by unexpectedly. It was hard to know who was more surprised at the unexpected drop-in ... Art, the other woman, or me.

Their persistence wasn't hard to understand. For one thing, Art was Art. For another, as soon as he and I became serious, he'd turned them off as though they were spigots.

But back to the letter out of his past.

It was a Friday, and we were in the cabin for the night drawing up the plans for each section of the first floor stud walls so we'd know how much lumber to order. The letter was on top of a pile of mail on the floor where we were sitting.

"Who's Laura X?" I asked, reading the name on the return address.

He looked up, puzzled, so I picked up the envelope and waved it at him.

"Oh," he said, "*Laura*." He shrugged. "Just someone I used to know."

He was trying to concentrate on the drawing, on placing the windows properly and counting how many 2x6s we'd need for the headers, and when he was concentrating on something it was often hard to get his full attention.

"Someone you used to know ... when?" I asked.

He looked up at me. "Huh?"

"When did you know her?" I waved the envelope again. "Laura?"

"Oh." He went back to the drawing. "A very long time ago."

And I knew that I could ask ten more questions and find out hardly anything more than I already knew. Did he think if he showed little or no interest in talking about it, then I would surmise it had been of no real interest to him even when he knew her?

But then his pencil stopped moving. "Oh," he said. He looked up.

"'Oh' what?" I said.

He put his pencil down. "I'd forgotten ... I think she's coming for a visit."

"Here?" I said. Now this was something unexpected.

"With her new husband," he added.

I nodded. I looked at the handwriting on the envelope. Fancy script. I had read somewhere that 'i's' with big circular dots over them indicated a big ego.

"When are they coming?" I asked.

Tima Smith

He raised his shoulders a little, let them fall, and then he frowned and I knew that something slightly alarming had occurred to him. "You better look at the letter," he said.

Gladly. I scanned the fancy writing with the big fat dots over all the 'i's'. *Hello dear Art ... she thought of him often. Building a house? Now that was something she had to see. Had he heard she'd married again? They were going to be in the area and would love to stop and visit...*

The first thing that occurred to me was the fact that it obviously wasn't always one-sided, this getting in touch. Because how else would she know where we were and that we were building a house?

I continued scanning: *... we'll be there on the 16th. Can't wait to see you after all this time ... much love ...*

The sixteenth. The sixteenth? "The SIXTEENTH?" I said, "but that's tomorrow! They're coming tomorrow! At ten-thirty in the morning!"

"Hmmm," he said. "I knew there was something I was going to tell you."

He was already back to figuring 2x6s. As if we weren't having company the very next morning at all. Company out of his past, for God's sake. And here I hadn't taken a shower or washed my hair in three days.

I looked at the letter again. "They want to take us out to lunch," I said. "At a restaurant!"

"Well," he said, without looking up, "that would be a logical place to go for lunch."

"But I have nothing to wear!" I looked around at the dark pile of boxes beyond the circle of light from the kerosene lamp. Somewhere in that pile was a box containing my good clothes, well, my *better* clothes at least, clothes I hadn't seen in months, and since I had no idea which box they were in, clothes I wasn't going to see by the next morning either.

Fifty Acres, More or Less

"You'll look better than anyone else in the restaurant no matter what you're wearing," he said. Oh, Art.

***

"This is the foundation." Art pointed to the rectangle of concrete. "And as soon as we compact the earth inside the foundation, we'll be able to start framing the first floor." He glanced at me and smiled. "Should be next week."

He'd already given them a tour of the septic system and the well and the underground utilities, all of which, of course, were invisible.

"Ooooh," Laura said. Almost everything Art told her seemed to delight her.

The new husband looked around at the woods, then up at the sky. "Wow," he said. "Very nice. Yes, very very nice."

"Well, there's still a lot of work to do," I said, "but someday we hope it really will be nice."

I liked the new husband. He was trying so hard to be interested and enthusiastic. Laura, on the other hand, had cast most of her attention on Art. Though from time to time I'd caught her studying me. Most likely trying to figure out 'why her?'.

Laura was pretty, very pretty, and very blonde, and very bubbly. Which surprised me, the bubbly part, because that was about the last thing I thought Art would be drawn to. She smelled nice. She was wearing jeans and a white silk blouse and cute little slip-on ballerina shoes that she was trying to keep clean.

"I thought I told you to wear your work clothes," Art said to her.

"Oh Art," she giggled, grabbing his arm and hugging him. "You know me. I'm not exactly a country girl!" Then she glanced at me. "Not like Tima!"

Tima Smith

I wouldn't have been surprised if I'd suddenly sprouted Pippi Longstocking pigtails and a gap between my front teeth. And I was achingly aware that I hadn't used conditioner on my hair in four months, that I was wearing a shirt with a frayed collar and pants with a hole just above one knee, that my fingernails were broken from working cement, and *my* shoes were sneakers … old, scuffed, run-down, and probably smelly.

"Well," the new husband said, coming to my rescue, "now that we've had a chance to be impressed by this amazing project of yours, how about if we top it off with a meal. Our treat."

He *was* a nice guy.

We went to an old inn Art and I had heard about … a former carriage stop, vintage New England. I fingered the linen table napkin, leaned forward to smell the flowers in the centerpiece, listened to the clink of ice cubes as the waitress poured the water. What I really wanted in that moment was to live there until someone came and announced that the house was finished and I could come home now.

"So," Laura said, smiling at me, "how did you two meet, anyway?"

"At Brandeis," I said. "I was taking Art's writing class and …"

"Oh Art!" she said, "do you remember that class with…" and she was off reminiscing.

I sipped my deliciously icy water. The new husband and I listened for a while, but we didn't know Professor Dunbar and weren't particularly interested in the way he lisped, or the way Laura couldn't understand a thing he said (even without the lisp, I wondered?), and so we started our own conversation, trying to find some common threads.

The lunch, I have to say, was delicious and the service impeccable. And through it all, Laura talked. Endlessly endlessly talked. Every once in a while, Art would say "Un-huh" and then she'd be off again. She talked through dessert, through coffee and tea, through the clearing of the table, until finally Art pushed his chair back and said, "It's been a wonderful visit, a wonderful lunch, and I for one could sit here all afternoon, but it's time for us to let you go on with your travels."

In the front seat, she talked all the way back to the hill, and I'm pretty sure she was still talking as we waved them off down the driveway.

"One thing," I said, smiling and waving, "how ever did she know where you were and what you were doing?" I glanced sideways at him, shrugged. "Just out of curiosity?"

"She and Benjamin have always kept in touch," he said. "I guess he's been keeping her up on what's going on."

I nodded. Benjamin. The friend with no tact and the negative opinions on our 'tangent.' "She's nice," I said, "and I really liked her new husband."

He put his arm around me. "Listen," he said.

I listened. "I don't hear anything," I said.

"That's the point," he said.

I looked at him and raised my eyebrows in an unspoken question.

He shrugged. "Some things simply have no explanation. Maybe I just wasn't very smart back then." And he touched my cheek. "Not like now." Then he grabbed my hand and pulled me toward the foundation. "So what do you say we get those last two sills on this afternoon." It was fine with me. At that moment everything was fine with me.

***

We've always thought we should have given out at least two prizes — one for the most thoughtless and one for the most thoughtful visitor remark. The former would have gone to someone who announced as she was getting out of her car, "Well, I

Tima Smith

mean, you drive by places like this, but you never think anyone actually *lives* there!"

But then that would be balanced out by a visitor who had a very different take. "My God," he kept saying, "it's beautiful!" He was an architect acquaintance who'd just finished walking from unfinished room to unfinished room shortly after we'd finally *finally* moved in.

He loved it. We do, too.

Fifty Acres, More or Less

VI

I woke up one morning and I couldn't breathe. Physically. I couldn't get air. I thought I was going to die. Then I breathed. The feeling I was going to die, though, that stayed. Until I couldn't stand it anymore and I told him he was suffocating me, that I couldn't stay married to him anymore.

We'd come close to splitting up six years earlier and he'd written me a letter saying he understood. That if I gave him a chance, he'd do better. He'd grow up. Start being a father. And he said if it didn't work or it wasn't enough, he would leave. Or I could have a life outside our marriage, if that's what I wanted. He'd do anything if he could at least stay for a while.

The letter made me feel selfish. And it also made me feel hopeful. I carried it in my wallet for years. Even long after he was gone. But the thing is, nothing changed. He wasn't better, wasn't a good father. For him, intent was enough all by itself.

But this time, I wasn't going to settle for intent. I was way beyond that. There was nothing left ... I didn't like him, I didn't respect him, I didn't admire him in any way. In fact, I had no feeling of any sort. He seemed to get it this time. He asked me for another chance to at least be a father. He said he needed to be alone with the kids. And because our business was in the barn behind the house, we made a plan. If I left during the week. He'd leave on weekends. It sounded like a first step toward something. Not ideal, but what would be? Perhaps it was as close to reasonable as we were going to get.

The first Friday I came home, all the locks had been changed. The shock of the next three months is inside me like a brick even after all this time. I was punished, humiliated, accused. How did I dare to not want him anymore. I carried the guilt of my traumatized children like a massive lump of lead. It was my fault. I'd tried to change my life and created havoc instead. It never occurred to me that for once he might have put someone beside himself first.

Tima Smith

CHAPTER TWELVE

Going Up

As is common in passive solar houses, the square footage of our original plan was small, about 1200 square feet. We'd chosen a simple, saltbox-style with an open first floor — a kitchen, an L-shaped living room with the ell on the east end and an eating area at the west end, a utility room, and a half-bath. The second floor was going to be smaller than the first, with the saltbox-style roof clipping off about a third of the north/south first floor dimension. It would accommodate two bedrooms and a full bath, not really enough for our family, but that was the plan. Art and I would get one bedroom, Lauren the other, and we really didn't know what we were going to do with Brian, who'd be spending all his school breaks at home — although there was some vague talk of making the living room ell into his space. For a long time we weren't sure about what to do with that ell, and it would take fifteen years before we finally finished it off with a big window seat as a reading area. It functioned as a work area until then, housing the table saw and surrounded by plastic drapes which were supposed to keep the tons of dust the saw produced out of the rest of the house, but didn't.

Framing the first floor was like getting the green flag after too many yellow laps. Finally, we were *going* someplace. It was terrific. And it wasn't the backbreaking work we'd been doing. It was relatively easy, straightforward and fast. The white 2x6 stud walls were beautiful, and all of a sudden we could see where there'd be doors, windows. Rooms!

We'd applied a termite shield to the top of the foundation, a thin aluminum sheet with a bent edge that protruded over the

Tima Smith

outside edge of the concrete. Supposedly, termites can't navigate from the underside of the aluminum to the top. I have no idea why. I also have no idea if it works, but it cost hardly anything and was easy to set in place.

Actually, we'd been told we needed more than just a termite shield. That a house on a slab required chemical termite treatment to avoid future problems. So we had someone come and give us an estimate on spraying the earth inside and surrounding the foundation. It wasn't a huge expense, but it was going to be a heavy application and the exterminator told us we should stay away from the area for a week after application.

We don't even like to use bug spray so we decided to avoid the poison and hope the termites stayed in the surrounding woods.

So far they have.

On top of the termite shield, we applied sill sealer, a thin layer of poly foam that goes between the top of the foundation and the wooden sill the walls are nailed to. It fills any spaces between the uneven concrete and the sill. Then we installed the sill, pressure-treated 2x6s, over the fastening bolts we'd embedded in the top of the concrete foundation wall before it set.

We'd decided to build with 2x6s instead of the usual 2x4s and place the studs every twenty-four inches instead of every sixteen. The thicker walls would accommodate the heavier insulation we planned to use, 6 1/4 inch thick with an R-value of 19. That depth of insulation, with three-quarter-inch plywood on the outside covered with 1" tongue-and-groove rigid insulation board was supposed to allow vapor on the inside of the house to pass through the fiberglass, through the plywood, and through the insulation board before condensing and turning to water. We wanted to be sure that vapor turned to water *out*side the house, not halfway through the wall, where it could eventually cause rot.

It took about two weeks to frame the exterior walls and finish the first floor ceiling and the second-floor deck.

Fifty Acres, More or Less

We used shiplap pine for the first floor ceiling, and I stained all the boards before we nailed them in place. Then, to act as a sound-deadening material between the shiplap first floor ceiling and the 2" tongue and groove pine we laid as the floor for the second level, we put down a layer of homosote. Homosote comes in 1/2"x4'x8' sheets. It's composed of many layers of paper and glue and it's indestructible. The more it's exposed to moisture, the harder it gets, and although we didn't know it at the time, it was going to be exposed to inches and inches of moisture — rain, snow, sleet, you name it.

By the time we were laying the second level floor, it was nearing the middle of October, crisp and sunny. The foliage was beginning to turn. Art had started teaching in Cambridge two days a week, and Lauren was in school all day. But things were moving along well, and somehow it seemed as though the worst was behind us.

Now, everything we did showed, and it didn't seem like such a big deal ... putting the structure up, enclosing it, getting it weather-proof. *That* was our goal — to have a tight house around us before winter hit. Then we'd put all our energy into finishing off the interior.

By now, we'd been atop the hill for five months, and one thing we'd discovered was that our driveway was something akin to a moat. Most people chose not to even try driving up. Half of those who did, changed their minds part-way and backed down. Though some, mostly men, seemed to take it as a personal challenge, sacrificing mufflers, catalytic converters, entire exhaust systems to those protruding water bars.

If a person's reason for coming was significant enough or if a hike straight uphill was the kind of exercise that didn't phase them, then they walked. But that was rare. And they weren't always happy when they arrived at the top. Over the years, FedEx and UPS have driven up one time each, after which they arranged to leave things at the bottom with a neighbor. I can only guess what the inside of those trucks looked like and how many 'fragile' packages didn't make it.

So ... there I was one afternoon, alone, nailing flooring boards on the second level when I heard voices. At first I thought it was my imagination. The voices got louder. Had someone left a radio on? Not that either. I stopped hammering, sat back, and gaped at two older women who were walking up the driveway. They were chattering away at each other, seemingly not bothered in the least by their climb, not gasping, not red-faced. And when they saw me they called out and waved. My god, they were cheerful.

They thought I was exactly what I looked like, a construction worker. "Is the owner here?" they asked.

"Sorry, no," I said, deciding for some reason to keep a low profile. If they were selling something, I didn't want to have to listen, and I certainly didn't want to stop working and climb down.

One of them waved a brochure. "We'll just leave this then," she said, and she put the brochure on a stack of lumber. Then they called good-bye and waved and started back down the driveway still chattering away.

Jehovah Witnesses.

They'd been following me all my life.

***

Standing on top of that second floor deck, ten feet off the ground, the view was amazing. And almost as soon as we first stood there, it occurred to us that inserting a full-sized second floor between the first floor and a half-sized third floor might be a very good idea. It was a moment when lightning should have flashed or a sudden great wind come to knock us down and bang our brains back to normal. But there was no lightning, no wind, only a consideration that for the next two years, there were going to be at least three of us living here. Four, five, or six during summers and vacations, and eight when everybody visited.

Fifty Acres, More or Less

I was used to living with five kids and all the accompanying noise, commotion, and activity. But for Art, there'd only been two, and since Michael had moved away, he'd had his house all to himself. I could write anywhere, work under any conditions, but Art needed peace and quiet or he couldn't concentrate. If we enlarged the house, we reasoned, we'd not only gain room on the second floor for an extra bedroom and a laundry, but a partial third floor that would provide a private space for writing and an even more-than-dynamite view. Not to mention the potential for extra bedroom space when it was needed.

The framing on the first floor had gone so quickly, how could adding a floor possibly be a bad idea?

If only my future self could have intervened and given my then-present self a good swift kick.

"It will almost double your cost," my future self would have told me. "It will mean the top of your roof is thirty-five feet off the ground instead of twenty-six, and you're afraid of heights. It means fifteen years from now, the house *still* won't be finished. And it means you're going to spend this entire winter living outdoors!"

Well, that would have been my pessimistic future self. My optimistic future self might have pointed out that kids would be moving in and out of the house for years, one leaving, two returning as if on cue. That grandchildren would live there and have enough room to race around without bumping into each other or anyone else. That for the first time in my life I'd have bedrooms big enough to allow getting up on either side of the bed, storage space galore, closets that weren't jammed tight, a room just for exercise. And views to knock your socks off from every window.

Listening to those two future selves, I can't be absolutely certain which way I'd have gone, but I tend to think I would have thought my pessimistic self was just being a great big fat pain in the ass.

So we went up, and up.

***

Tima Smith

As things go, most of the wonder of framing the first floor wore off sometime during the framing of the second. For one thing, it was getting colder and colder. Art wasn't only gone two days a week, he had to spend a significant amount of time on his students' papers. My kids were knee deep in school or work and had hardly any spare time to help. And it was getting dark earlier and earlier. Plus, I think we were getting just plain tired.

Things slowed way down.

I remember having the impression that it didn't seem to matter how many wall sections we banged together every day, because the number we still had to do seemed to be multiplying. It was as if we weren't just standing still, but losing ground. And of course the farther off the ground we got, the more difficult everything became.

We had no stairs to the second floor yet, just an eight-foot wooden ladder, and everything had to be carried or handed up.

So just when we needed things to move faster, it all went in the exact opposite direction.

***

Then it was November. Gray skies, stark bare trees, days full of thin sunlight. The color of fall was lying on the ground and it was often too cold to work bare-handed. The second floor stud walls were trickier to put up than the first, mainly because the tops were eighteen feet off the ground. To avoid having to carry sheets of heavy plywood up a ladder and hold them in place while they were nailed, we sheathed the exterior of the walls before they went up, which made each wall heavier, harder to control.

When it was time to raise a wall, I could never get myself to push it past a certain angle. Straight up didn't feel straight up, it felt as if the wall was going straight over the edge, along with everyone holding onto it. So while Art was pushing it up, I'd be pulling it back, and more than a few times he had to yell at me to let go.

Not that we ever did lose a wall over the edge, but in the pit of my stomach I felt the possibility every time we set one in place.

As fall slid into winter, there were times when I simply froze, not from the cold, but from utter confusion. There were windows to install on the first floor, a chimney to be built, second floor walls to raise, plywood and insulation board to be applied to the first floor exterior, a staircase to be built from the first to the second floor. Not to mention a third floor and a roof.

But we were fast running out of money, so shouldn't I have been writing and trying to sell stories? But how could I concentrate on *that* when the clock was running down on the season and there was still so much to do?

Somehow, it never really hit me until it was already upon us that winter was going to beat *us* instead of the other way around.

That full-sized second floor that had been such a good idea just weeks ago truly seemed to have a spell on it. The exterior walls *were* endless, and we were beginning to feel hopelessly overwhelmed. Then Brian showed up one cold weekend morning with Chris Barry and Pat Cloney, two friends from college. He'd said they were coming to lend a hand, but when they arrived and Chris said hello and strapped on his tool belt, there was something about the way he did it that made me see Clint Eastwood in a *Fistful of Dollars*. This guy knew what he was doing.

Chris took over, didn't ask a question, just gave directions, and the fact that we didn't have to make decisions, that we could just follow along like good little workers was almost as good as a weekend in Hawaii.

The entire second floor was framed by the end of the day, including some of the interior walls of the bedrooms. It almost made me giddy.

After they left, Art wondered if Brian might have actually paid his friend for that incredible day's work. I never asked, but if you did Brian, it was a great gift. And if you didn't, it was still a great gift.

Tima Smith

VII

He took it for twelve weeks, and then he left. He didn't say he was leaving for good, he said he'd be away for two weeks and needed me to stay with the kids, that he had some business to take care of. He sounded almost pleasant. As though he'd come to terms with everything.

I needed to believe that because all I wanted was to be home with my kids again, even if it were only for two weeks, for any time at all. Surely, he had come to his senses. The three months of hell, a lawyer so sleazy he was more like a caricature, threats and accusations, and me with no money, NO money — surely that was over now, a kind of terrible adult tantrum that had run its course.

Art and I had become friends. Not close yet, but getting closer, which was wonderful, and I was back home and the nightmare was over. There was the writing and there was Art and the kids and I were together and during the first week I was home, the bank called to tell me the mortgage hadn't been paid in three months. Neither, I discovered when the lights went out, had the electric bill or any other bills. I stopped answering the business phone because everyone was calling to find out why their orders hadn't been delivered. Then the sleazy lawyer called looking for my ex, who had paid him with a check that bounced. That's how I found out there was nothing in any of the bank accounts, either. Still, it was one of the few satisfying conversations I had that week. "So, join the club," I told him and hung up.

CHAPTER THIRTEEN

That Game-Changing Third Floor

By early December, the 2x12 stringers for the third-level floor were in place. Now we needed the third-level walls and a roof, but winter had already decided not to extend us a grace period. There'd been flurries. It was regularly below freezing every morning. My plants were long dead. There were no more luke-warm showers. We'd been at it non-stop for eight months. We were tired, probably run-down from our lousy diet of Kudos and salad and pecan pie. It began to feel like we were part of a bad dream. And it was never far from our minds that if we'd kept the original plan and stuck to two floors, we just might already have had a roof over our heads.

We put up giant blue tarps across the tops of the second floor walls. They made the place eerily dark, but gave the impression of enclosure. Then we had one big wet snowstorm and every little sag in the tarps swelled. Finally the plastic ripped from the nails and caved in. We shoveled. The snow melted. We swept the water out of the second floor and kept working.

In mid-December, there was a weather break, and Greg and Michael E and Grannis came for a weekend push on putting up the third floor walls. The third floor was two-thirds the size of the second, with only three exterior walls — north, east, and west.

If we could get those exterior walls up and if the weather stayed reasonable into January, we thought it might be possible to actually get a roof on. And if we got a roof on, and all the windows

Tima Smith

in, the house would be enclosed — water and snow-tight at least as much as the cabin.

We fantasized about getting a rough bathroom working. We'd have water, electricity, and perhaps with a couple of space heaters, we could live in just two rooms on the second floor. It was a desperate plan, but desperation was waiting just outside the door we hadn't built yet.

There was nothing in the budget for renting a house for the winter. We couldn't imagine living in the cabin during January and February. We had to get that roof on. We simply had to.

***

As far as the third floor was concerned, I was useless. It was a fear that was entirely consistent. I had a height limit of about eighteen feet, whether I was inside the structure or outside on a ladder, as though I had a kind of atmospheric alarm that allowed me to climb so high and no higher. It turned out that Grannis had even less tolerance for height than I, so while Art and Greg and Michael E braved the third floor, Grannis and I got busy filling in gaps in plywood siding and applying the exterior rigid insulation board as high as we could get ourselves to climb.

We still had no stairs. To get to the second floor, you had to climb an eight-foot wooden ladder all the way to the top, to the part the safety stickers say NEVER to stand on, then take one good-sized step up onto the edge of the opening for the staircase. To get to the third floor, we had an aluminum extension ladder in one of the bedrooms.

There was no plywood nailed over the 2x12 stringers on the third-level floor, although there were a few loose sheets you could move around depending on where you needed something relatively solid to stand on. But mainly, you had to walk on the edges of the 2x12s to get from here to there, and the edge of a 2" board isn't really 2 inches, it's 1 1/2 inches. And the stringers were spaced two feet apart. Just thinking about it makes me go a little weak.

The third-floor east and west gable end walls were 13 feet high at their peak and 20 feet long. Even Greg, who was as strong as any three of us and seemed to have been absent when they handed out the fear gene, wasn't particularly excited about putting them in place. He decided it should be done in two stages. The first stage would consist of an eight-foot high stud wall, and when each of those was nailed and braced, then the top sections would be added.

The second-floor walls had gone up in sections ten or twelve feet long by eight feet high. They were big, but controllable. The gable walls for the third floor were longer by eight feet, a significant increase in 2x6s and exterior plywood, a significant increase in weight. And even though each side was lightened somewhat by two seven foot tall by two foot wide openings for those Cambridge windows, they were still heavy walls being set in place twenty feet off the ground.

There were exterior wooden stops nailed in place at the top of the second-floor wall to keep the third-floor walls from going over, but it was obvious to me that if one of those walls got out of control, the stops weren't going to stop them, just slow them down before the inevitable plunge.

They banged the walls together, nailed on the plywood, decided who was going to do what, counted to three and heaved. The walls went up. They didn't fall over. Three people held them, while someone ran around like crazy nailing them in place, though what I'm saying is only hearsay, because I couldn't watch.

The rear third-floor wall was a snap. Thirty-six feet long and only six feet high, it was a manageable wall that went up quickly in three twelve-foot sections, with outer plywood attached. Instant enclosure. There'd be no front wall because the front of the saltbox roof was going to sit on the top of the second-level front wall. The only front wall we were going to need on the third floor would be an interior wall to separate the third floor from the two south-facing bedrooms on the second floor, and that wall would wait for a long long time.

The top sections of the two gable-end walls were frightening. Brian had to be called, because they needed to be carried up from the inside on ladders with two people on each end, then set on top of the bottom sections, their peaks approximately 36 feet off the ground.

In preparation, the exterior plywood on the bottom sections of these walls extended up above their top edge about a foot or two. This gave the top sections something to butt against, a mini-wall to help hold each top section in place until it was nailed to the bottom section and braced. It also insured that the sections would be well-tied together and stiffened by the plywood.

From the ground, those walls seemed to soar straight into the sky.

Somehow, all the third floor walls went up that weekend. And we must still have been in possession of some well of optimism, because everyone pledged to meet again the following weekend, as long as the weather held, to get the roof started.

So much for optimism.

Our December weather break ended twenty-four hours later with snow, then sleet, then icy rain. All we could do was wait and wonder if we were going to be roofless until spring.

***

As far as the cabin went, people ask why we didn't winterize it once we realized that was where we were going to spend the winter. And really, I don't know the answer. Except I think by then we were a little deranged by it all. It seemed ridiculous to us to be spending time and money on the cabin when there was still so much to do in the house. And by then, the house had become a sort of mad obsession. Doing anything that took time or resources away from it was simply unimaginable. So we slid into camping out all winter, got used to it, accepted it.

At least the cabin had a roof, a kerosene heater to warm your hands by, a sofa bed to sleep on, and a wooden floor instead of dirt.

***

And so the summer of the Big Dig, which brought the Heavy Downpours that washed the sand out of The Trench From Hell over and over again, was followed by the Winter of Wet Snow and Big Winds. The Big Winds started as soon as the third-floor walls reached thirty-five feet into the air, unattached to a roof. And The Big Winds seemed to come only when Lauren and I were alone, when Art was off in Cambridge, and at night.

Up at the top of the hill, a big wind comes through the trees sounding like a freight train. No, I lie. It actually sounds like a *host* of freight trains. The really high winds always come from the same direction, from behind the house, from north-northeast, and you can hear them coming, roaring, before they break into the clearing and womp the house.

Today, with the house insulated and tight, the sound is much diminished, although because the house is tall, it still takes the wind on the chin. If the winds are more than sixty-miles-per-hour, the house creaks. If they're more than seventy miles per hour, sometimes it will shudder. I always breathe a sigh of relief when October comes and goes and the hurricane season is over. So far, we've been lucky. No big ones to test our roof tie-down system or our roofing shingle application.

Sometimes I wonder what it would be like up here with a repeat of the only severe hurricane I ever experienced, Carol in the 1950s, or that terrible hurricane of 1938. Would I stay and ride out the storm? I don't know. Art does. He says he'd stay. But I don't know if I'm brave enough for that, now that I know a roof can act like a sailplane and the wind can knock a house right off its foundation.

Tima Smith

I do know this: that first winter, when there was nothing between us and the freight train but a thin 3/4" plywood wall, the wind was a noise you felt in your stomach and on the back of your neck. A huge noise that made you understand what it must have felt like to lie awake listening to the wolves and saber-toothed tigers prowling outside the mouth of the cave.

***

Weather-wise, the worst night, at least for me, started off innocently enough. Art was in Boston. Lauren and I were together in her trailer. We had an evening ritual by then. Every evening just after dusk, a half a dozen mice emerged from wherever it was they spent their days, always emerging *into* the trailer first, perhaps on the chance that we'd set a little mouse smorgasbord for them.

They poked their heads out from various spots to see if the coast was clear, and we did our level best to convince them it was not. We banged pots, stomped the floor, yelled 'Get out of here' to make them disappear. Which they always did within seconds. Then you'd hear them scurrying down through the bowels of the trailer to the outside, where they'd have to make due with frozen seeds and berries and whatever else mice manage to live on in December.

We didn't want to snap their necks in a trap or poison them, so we'd learned to take the damn things in stride, and on this one memorable evening Lauren was studying while I listened to the six o'clock news. I paid close attention to weather reports, hoping for a December warm-up, but that night the weather person wasn't talking thaw, she was predicting a storm, with sixty-mph winds and even higher gusts.

It had been dark out since four that afternoon, but I glanced out the trailer window toward the house, thinking about the third floor with those free-standing walls nailed only at the bottom and held vertical by a 2x16 brace every eight feet.

I called Greg in Massachusetts.

He listened and didn't come right back at me with his usual, "Don't worry about it, Mum, it's no big deal." Instead, he hit me with a silence that went on too long. Finally he said, "You've got to put on more bracing. Use the longest pieces you can find and tie the walls to the floor rafters in as many places as you can."

"Okay," I said.

"And use big nails," he added.

I suppose I could have asked Lauren for help. And she would have. But the thought of worrying about *her* up there in the dark, in addition to myself, didn't seem worth it. Besides, right or wrong, I couldn't help feeling that she hadn't asked for any of this, only *I* had.

So I pulled on my boots.

"I'm going up on the third floor," I said. "If I'm not back in forty-five minutes, you can have all my clothes."

She didn't say anything, but her look said, "Very funny."

There were lots of times that winter when I felt sorry for myself. But that night I was wallowing. I had to do the two things I hated most. Go up high and walk around on those two-inch rafter edges. And I had to do it in the dark.

I went through the house with a flashlight looking for the longest 2x3s and 2x4s I could find, sixteen-footers, twelve-footers. I had to get them up to the second floor, lean them against the third floor stairwell, climb the ladder and pull myself up first, then pull the braces up and carry each one to an outside wall, nail it in place as high as I could reach, then nail it to a floor rafter.

The wind was already picking up, and I had to juggle the flashlight and the boards and my mounting fear. The flashlight beam cast arcing shadows across the stud walls, the voids of the window holes, the ladders and the tools and the piles of cut stud ends lying all around. How could this cold, dark, vacant space ever be a warm, inviting home, I wondered. Everything we did was like trying to fill a bucket one drop at a time.

Tima Smith

I kicked over a can of eight-penny nails and didn't care. At that moment, it was all hopeless. Our intentions, insane. Our goal, beyond reach. We'd put everything we had into this gray hulk of a building, and it had eaten it up as though all our time and effort had been nothing.

It wasn't a house, it was a pit, a sinkhole, and that night, I was sure I had nothing more left to lose to it.

But at the same time, I seemed to have no knowledge of anything else. There was no second choice, nothing waiting at the next corner. No rational, easy way forward. But no rational, easy way out either.

I could hear the wind. Not a roar yet, but I knew it soon would be. I ignored it, tried to focus instead on moving one board at a time up one ladder, then up the next.

The only way I could nail was to hold the flashlight in the crook of my neck, the light ricocheting everywhere. It made for a lousy aim, so it took a long time. And I did most of it on the verge of tears.

By the time I'd used up all the bracing I could find, by the time I'd nailed them all in place, by the time I'd climbed down, the wind beginning a low howl, my nerves were stretched as far as they'd go. I really didn't give a damn if the walls *did* come crashing down.

I stuck my head in the trailer and told Lauren I was going to bed, walked the cold dark path to the cabin, and put a pillow over my ears so I wouldn't have to hear that damn wind. Eventually I fell asleep.

The next morning the sky was blue and innocent. There were broken limbs and tree branches everywhere. I was a little afraid to look, but the third floor walls were exactly where they'd been the night before. So I ate two Kudos and went to work.

***

Today, I'm sure we did everything we could to make the house stand up to severe weather. We installed oversized j-bolts to hold the sill onto the foundation. The plywood siding spans wall sections rather than beginning and ending at the top and bottom of each. And the roof rafters are not merely notched and toe-nailed into the tops of the walls but doubly tied down with metal straps, Art's idea, and he attached every one.

Tima Smith

VIII

But there was money. I knew that. Or at least there was supposed to be. It was the house mortgage refinance. The final payment for the boat. Half of the total price. Fifty thousand dollars. And it was in my name and each of my children's. Five, ten-thousand-dollar treasury bills. But when I found the paperwork and checked on it, the treasury bills had matured and been cashed. That money was gone. Every cent. Five checks cashed with what appeared to be my signature on the back. Except I hadn't signed them.

When I got copies of the checks and stared at the signature, I recognized the handwriting. My mother-in-law had signed my name on those checks. Did she have the money?

When I went to the bank, I was told that it was a federal crime to have cashed those checks illegally. So I filled out a form charging my ex with a federal crime and the FBI was called. They would be in touch.

In the meantime, I had an entirely new set of problems. A letter arrived from the bank that held the mortgage on the house threatening foreclosure if the several thousand dollars in arrears was not paid immediately. They wanted to see me. I didn't have several thousand or even several hundred dollars and I called and made an appointment to talk to them.

I expected the bank to be very no-nonsense. I expected to hear very bad news. But the young man I spoke with the next day at the bank was unusually courteous. After we sat down, he seemed to pull himself together for a moment and then asked me if I knew a woman named ___. I told him yes. I told him she was my mother-in-law. He said she had called that week to tell them that I was irresponsible, had no money, and couldn't possibly pay the mortgage on my home. He asked her, he said, if she would be willing to help. She said no and suggested that the bank foreclose on me immediately.

We sat there, he and I, staring at each other. "She told you to foreclose on me?" I repeated. He nodded.

So she knew that the mortgage hadn't been paid, that foreclosure was in the offing. Knew that her son had put us in this situation, one she apparently approved of. And it occurred to me for the first time that he wasn't coming back in two weeks, most probably wasn't coming back at all.

What, I wondered, had this woman been all those years I'd known her as a loving grandmother to my children? A latent Machiavelli?

"You have five children?" the bank man said. I nodded. "She's their grandmother?" I nodded again. He shook his head. "We're not going to foreclose," he said. "Especially after a phone call like that."

Instead, he asked for an amount each month that was less than the mortgage amount, but not exactly a small amount. I told him I would do that. Even though I had no idea how. It was the second explosion in an insanity that would go on far too long.

Tima Smith

CHAPTER FOURTEEN

The Longest, Most Terrible, Most Horrible, Most Miserable Winter

The weather was wretched through the end of December and into January, and we were disheartened knowing that it would be spring before we could hope to get a roof on the place.

But we kept working.

We still had windows to install, and we had to finish the interior walls on the second floor. We couldn't do the first floor interior walls until we set the masonry floor, and we couldn't do the floor until we could count on warmer weather.

For Christmas, the whole family received an invitation from my brother and his wife to come to their house in Massachusetts.

Walking into their home, I felt like Alice stepping through the looking glass. Everything was super-real. The air inside the house wasn't the same temperature as the air outside, it was warm, and that actually surprised me. I sat on soft, comfortable, clean furniture. Things smelled good. And there was wonderful hot food, and interesting conversation.

Of course people asked how the house was coming, and we smiled and said it was coming along just fine. No one there could possibly have understood what we were doing or how we were living. For people who thought that scraping an inch of ice off their car windshields was a terrific annoyance, our life style was too crazy to comprehend.

I remember not wanting to leave, not wanting to return to the dark, cold, ungracious world we lived in. And when we finally did, the driveway had iced over and we all had to walk up the hill in the dark, slipping and sliding, Jennifer in her high heels somehow beating us all.

But instead of being ultimately depressing, that day away helped. It said there was something beyond the place we were stuck in, and someday we might have a bit of that bright, warm, graceful space back again.

Tima Smith

IX

 When an FBI agent called about the check-cashing fraud, he asked me to meet him at the police station in Brockton, MA. It was a big brick, several-story building in the middle of a city that hadn't seen a good day since the 1960s. The agent was a clean-cut, well-dressed man about my age. He took me upstairs into an area the size of a small ballroom. There were two policemen in plain clothes, detectives I assumed, chatting near the front of the room, and the agent and I sat down at a table at the far end. He wasted no time getting to the point.

 He told me they did not believe my accusation. That it was their opinion that my ex-husband and I were attempting to 'double our money' and that what we were doing was a serious federal crime punishable by a lengthy time in jail for both of us, or at least for me, since my ex was missing.

 The air went thin. This was nothing remotely close to what I'd expected. I sat there trying to process what he was saying. Then, at the other end of the room, there was a commotion. It grew loud enough so that despite what was happening where I was sitting, I couldn't ignore it. When I glanced over, a woman began to yell at the two detectives, growing more frantic by the second. She was holding something in her hand, waving it around. I looked back at the FBI agent to judge his reaction. Did she really have a hand grenade? You certainly couldn't tell by the look on his face. He was undisturbed enough for me to think for a split-second that I was having a major hallucination. She yelled that she was going to "kill everyone in this fucking building. You let the fucking murderers walk around out there," she yelled, "and you arrest my husband when he did nothing wrong! I'm going to blow this fucking place to dust!"

 I felt sick to my stomach. Was this really happening?

 The FBI agent seemed to be studiously ignoring it. "Do you see what's going on over there?" I said to him. He nodded. "If I say to," he told me, "get under the table." Under the table, I thought. Was this the way the world was going to go for the rest of my life?

Fifty Acres, More or Less

The two detectives kept talking to the woman, calmly, trying to talk her down, which, after a while, they did. Was it a real hand grenade? I have no idea. And if it was, the pin mustn't have been pulled, because how could the detectives remain so calm? As though she were doing nothing more than offering them a cup of coffee and a doughnut, neither of them showing one iota of concern or panic.

The room went very quiet as they took her away. What next? I wondered. And then it came. The agent pushed a single piece of paper across the table to me. "If you sign this right now," he said, "we'll forget the whole thing. You can go home as if you'd never made the charge in the first place. You have five children. If you go to jail, who's going to take care of them?"

I listened to his words. My mind raced. I looked at the paper and read it. It began with 'I, Tima Smith' and then consisted of three statements. In the first, I was confessing to having filed a false charge. In the second, it stated that I was hereby withdrawing that false charge. In the third, it stated that any federal charges pending against me over the false charge I had made would be nullified.

I read it three times.

I thought about my kids. And for a moment, I even considered signing it. Just to be rid of this whole insane situation. But the main thing I focused on was admitting to having told a lie when I didn't. To having made a false accusation when I hadn't. And suddenly, I was pushing it back across the table to him. "I can't sign this," I said. "It's not true."

He looked at me for a second and I looked back, wondering what I'd just done. He shook his head, put the paper into his briefcase. "All right," he said, "you'll have to be fingerprinted and photographed and then you'll hear from us."

Sometimes when I look back at this, I wonder why it never occurred to me that they might just arrest me then and there. But they didn't. I was photographed, fingerprinted, and I went home. In a daze. Shaky and unbelieving. Had the world simply tipped on its axis? Or was it just me?

CHAPTER FIFTEEN

THE ROOF

In early January, a thaw set in. The air warmed into the 40s, the sky was clear and blue, there were no storms in the three-day forecast.

We already had the roof rafter installation planned out. All we'd been waiting for, hoping for, were two or three decent days. And it looked as if we were going to get them.

Greg called to say he could come for Saturday and Sunday. We called Jerry and begged him to come up from the Cape. And Michael E and Grannis would come down from Vermont.

For the front section of the roof, there were nineteen 2"x12"x24' rafters. We'd already notched them at the bottom ends where they'd sit on the top plate of the second-floor front wall, and they were also notched eighteen feet above that, where they'd sit on the crossbeam, an 8"x12"x 36' laminated beam that would eventually mark the top of the third floor interior front wall. The ends of this crossbeam sat on the side walls and on two evenly spaced upright third-floor center posts. In turn, these center posts sat on two upright second-floor posts, which sat on the two 12x12 salvaged pine posts on the first floor.

The nineteen 2"x12"x16' rafters for the rear of the roof were notched on one end only, the end that would sit on the rear third-floor wall. One set of rafters, either the front or the rear, would be offset by 1 1/2" so the two sets would snug against each other at the peak of the roof, where they would be nailed together. We'd consulted Charlie Wheedon, a local builder, about the roof design.

He'd okayed it with the stipulation we use five sixteen-penny nails when attaching the rafters at the peak. He said that each sixteen-penny nail was good for one hundred pounds of weight, and calculated that each rafter needed to bear five hundred pounds of roof and snow load. We put in six.

Art, Jerry and Greg did the up-in-the air stuff. Jerry straddled the front wall acting like he was twenty inches off the ground instead of twenty feet. Art and Greg were higher up, manning the crossbeam. Michael E, not a fan of heights, did the mid-level passing of the rafters. Grannis and I fed each rafter to him from the ground.

The first one or two rafters went up slowly and awkwardly, but then the roof crew got into a rhythm and started moving along fairly rapidly. The sight of those long white boards soaring into a clear blue sky was damn impressive.

It was a lot of work to do in one day, and by the time the last front rafter went up at dusk, Grannis and I barely had enough strength to get it vertical against the wall. Nineteen twenty-four foot 2x12s weigh a lot, even when you're only carrying one at a time.

Still in our work clothes, we took everyone out to dinner at the local best-pecan-pie-in-the-world restaurant. We were all exhausted and starving, and although everyone at the table deserved champagne, they got Coca-Cola and didn't seem to mind.

Because the front rafters were longer than the rear rafters, we thought the worst of the job was over. But despite their shorter length, it turned out that the rear roof rafters were actually more difficult to set in place. There was no supporting beam to rest them on, so each one had to be held in place at the peak while they were nailed to the front rafters with those six nails. Plus, the temperatures plummeted all that second day. The thaw had been short-lived.

By Sunday night, we were all too well aware of the tremendous amount of work we'd done. But we weren't satisfied yet. All we needed now was one more clear weekend to get the plywood in place and we'd have enough of a roof to keep out most of the snow and ice and rain that would surely come over the next two or three months.

The following weekend, Greg and Brian arrived early, and by Sunday evening, with the exception of a couple of feet on either side of the peak, the roof was covered with 5/8" CDX. Having most of a roof meant we could start working on interior things we'd been unable to do until then. All we had to do was make it through the rest of January and then through February. March sounded hopeful. Plus there was a chance, if the weather backed off, that we might even be able to shingle the roof and make the house truly snow and watertight for the remainder of the winter.

We should have been content to count ourselves lucky at what we'd been able to accomplish despite the fact it was January. At least then we wouldn't have suffered such a let-down. Because right after the roof plywood went on, winter set in with a vengeance.

It wasn't a winter like the three previous, mild and with little snow, but a winter with snow banks big enough to tunnel through and cold that settled in your bones. We needed to keep moving, had to keep our concentration on the seven thousand things we still had to do, but hibernation was preferable, and my memories of the rest of that January, all of February, and much of March are of fifty long cold gray days during which we accomplished hardly anything at all.

But the pictures show a different story.

The early April pictures, with the snow finally melting for good, show a house with windows and a front door and board and batten siding almost all the way up to the plywood roof. How, I still wonder, did we ever manage to do it?

Fifty Acres, More or Less

X

About a month after the grenade incident, my lawyer called and asked me to come in. He told me he'd heard from the FBI. The agent who'd urged me to sign a paper saying that my accusation was a lie now believed me and intended to support my suit to get the money my ex-husband had stolen. The FBI, my lawyer said, would prosecute my ex if they could find him. But that was doubtful, so instead, they would prosecute his mother. It was her handwriting on the checks. Did she own anything, the lawyer asked me ... a house? a car? Jewelry? Did she have bank accounts? No, she did not own a house. Yes, she owned a ten-year-old car. She had some jewelry, but what it was worth I had no idea. Bank accounts? I had no idea. But I doubted that she had anything close to fifty thousand dollars. She lived too carefully.

I sat there listening to what the lawyer was telling me. She could go to jail, the lawyer said, especially if she couldn't repay the money. She'd lose whatever she had. And it would be a long procedure with ugliness, accusation, denial, and expense.

It was true that I was in a terrible financial position. But I saw a better future. I had Art, a person I could count on, who I respected, admired, loved. My three oldest were going off to college next year. We'd be moving, and the younger two were going to have to adjust to a new place to live, a new school, new friends. In other words, we were moving forward with our lives, and it was going to take effort and focus. Yes, we needed the money, but at what cost? After everything that had happened, the fighting and the discord, I was exhausted. Sick of the stress, the negativity, the anger, the disappointment. Was it worth prolonging all that for the chance of walking away with something? Or, perhaps, nothing at all? Did I

Tima Smith

want to be responsible for a woman in her 60s being prosecuted by the FBI? Threatened with going to jail?

I considered it for a long time, and ultimately decided to let it go. I couldn't live in that old life any longer. What good would come of it? It would be nothing more than a protracted act of punishment. And it was going to mark me as much as the person I was punishing. I had to let it go for my own sake. It had to be over. And so it was.

CHAPTER SIXTEEN

A Plod

Despite the expansion of the second floor and the addition of the third, we had exactly the number of windows we needed. But because the old Andersons were unframed, each one required a lot of time to install: a frame had to be built, along with a sloped sill. Art did the windows because he was good at making things fit properly, careful and meticulous about measuring and cutting. I worked on less exacting things — building kitchen counters, the exterior siding, planning out the electric and plumbing.

I still remember walking into the first bedroom Art completed and seeing windows where there had only been empty gaps for so long. The windows are quite large, about four feet tall and three feet wide, with four horizontal panes on each casement. The graceful brass handles control a locking mechanism that pushes a rod up into the top of the frame and down into the bottom.

As far as I was concerned, each window gave as much grace to those unfinished rooms as hanging a Renoir.

While he worked on the windows, Art also got started on doors. He built an insulated wooden door for the west side of the house, our main entrance, and hung a set of Victorian double doors on the opposite wall. There was an opening for a second door on that northeast wall, where someday we wanted to build a deck. But we had no door for that yet and so all we did was plywood over the exterior and fill the space with insulation.

Little did we know that third doorway would stay that way for almost ten years.

Tima Smith

When the weather permitted, I concentrated on siding the exterior. We'd decided on board and batten, buying it from a local mill. The boards were approximately 10" wide, and we butted them as close as possible. But because the wood was green and would shrink, we'd still end up with spaces between each board, and that was the reason for the battens, which we nailed over the boards where they met. We'd ordered various length boards, from twelve to sixteen feet in order to stagger the seams. To be sure they'd shed water, we cut angles on the ends of each board so where two boards met one above the other, the angle on the low end of the top board met and covered the angle on the top end of the bottom board. Get it?

Putting up the siding was one of the most satisfying jobs we'd done to that point. For one thing, it wasn't difficult. Each board helped support the one above it, and even though they were green, they weren't particularly heavy or difficult to hold. Best of all, as the blue rigid insulation disappeared, the house started to look finished. Well, maybe not *finished*, but more like a house that was actually moving toward completion.

The only negative part of putting up the siding was clinching the 5000 nails that held it to the plywood sheathing. The sharp ends of most of those nails were visible on the inside, and we'd learned that it was a good idea to clinch them, so they wouldn't loosen and pull out with the expansion and contraction of the siding through the seasons. It wasn't a hard job, just terrifically boring.

***

It was about this time I actually voiced my doubts to Art about our being able to see the whole thing through. Yes, we'd accomplished a lot. After all, there was a three-story frame sitting in the clearing. But as we lay in bed every night talking about what needed to be done the next day and the day after that, the goal we were after, a habitable house, seemed to recede farther and farther away.

I'd say, "We need to mark where the walls will go for the utility room so we'll know where to put the breaker box."

And Art would say, "But we really can't do that until we have the breaker box and we know the size of the hot water heater and how much space we need for the upstairs plumbing and the downstairs bathroom."

"Right," I'd sigh, "right."

Every action we intended to take required seven other things to be done first, and several that we hadn't anticipated at all.

We were somewhere in the deep dark middle of something whose size we could only guess at.

"What are we doing?" I asked him one night. Lauren was a hundred yards away in her mouse-ridden trailer. We were in the cabin. The inside and outside temperature was somewhere about twenty-two degrees. I was fully dressed under the sleeping bag and the three comforters. Art was just wearing long underwear, but he was more impervious to the cold than I.

He didn't say anything for a second. Then he fished around under the covers until he found my hand. "What are we doing?" he repeated. "I think we're staring at the ceiling." But of course he knew what I was really asking.

"When I was in the army," he said, "because I was a fast runner, I was point man during basic training. Do you know what that is?"

I shook my head. "No."

"The point man's job," he said, "was to go ahead of his regiment and make sure the way was clear. In combat, that might mean getting shot first or being the one who stepped on a mine, but in training it meant opening a gate or standing on a bridge while everyone crossed."

Art has a wonderful voice, deep and resonant, and I was already feeling more relaxed just listening.

"If it was a gate, I closed it after the last man, and then had to get back to my position at the front. Which meant running past the

Tima Smith

whole regiment, maybe a hundred men, until I was ahead of them again and I could prepare for whatever it was they had to go over or under or through. You did it over and over until you were relieved. In full uniform, with a full pack and a rifle and…"

"You must have hated it," I said.

"That's just it," he said. "I didn't. I preferred it. It was tough, but it was a challenge, and the challenge was better than just marching along. Marching along was awful."

"So that's what we have here?" I said. "A challenge?"

"Well, we're not exactly marching along, are we."

"But there was purpose to that," I said, "to being a point man. It made sense. It had logic on its side."

"Which side is that?" he said. "War is the exact opposite of reason and sense and logic. If people acted reasonably, there'd be no reason for a point man. We find ourselves in situations that make no sense most of our lives. Would it make any more sense for both of us to be working forty hours a week to pay someone else to build our house at five times the cost? Or would it make more sense to decide we can't afford a house at all?" He squeezed my hand. "Remember that first day using the Case? When it lost *both* its tracks?"

I nodded. How could I forget.

"I never told you," he said, "but I was pretty sure we were cooked that day. For one thing, I didn't think we were going to be able to get those damn tracks back on, and if we couldn't do *that*, then how could we do the rest of it? But the thing is, you didn't act like that's what you were thinking at all. And *I* sure wasn't going to be the one to tell you it wasn't possible. And anyway, I was wrong. Because we did it. And mainly we did it because you seemed absolutely sure we could." He squeezed my hand again. "After that, I knew we could do this, too. And we have and we are and we will."

And then in typical fashion, after just a few seconds, I could tell by his breathing he was asleep.

Fifty Acres, More or Less

I lay there listening to the trees cracking in the frigid air, to the far-off sound of a truck running through its gears. Nearby, an owl hooted once, twice, and then an answer came from somewhere in the distance.

I knew Art had done hard things. In the Philippines and New Guinea. I knew he had a kind of strength that went much deeper than mere tissue. I'd seen it in his stoic response to his thyroid condition and to losing the sight in his eye. He was strong. He preferred a challenge to marching along with the column. Yes, he'd had doubts, but he'd kept them to himself because of what he perceived in me as confidence.

But it hadn't been confidence as much as naiveté.

I wasn't particularly strong or particularly stoic. So what, exactly was my contribution here? What hard things had I ever done?

The only thing that came to mind was the house I used to live in and the ten coats of paint that were peeling off all at once.

I'd gone outside one morning with a paint scraper and a heating iron and scraped an area maybe two feet square. Then I'd looked up at the rest of the wall, three stories high and fifty feet from front to back.

"This is ridiculous," I muttered, unplugging the iron and going back inside.

And it *was* ridiculous. Me, scraping the whole house alone. But when I got inside, I realized that no one else was going to do it, and I couldn't afford to hire anyone to do it for me, and if I didn't do it, it wasn't going to get done at all.

So I went back outside, plugged in the heater and set a goal of fifty square feet by lunchtime. And over two summers, the house got scraped fifty square feet at a time.

I watched a sliver moon pass across the icy window and it hit me that, if nothing else, I had perseverance. Enough to scrape a house, write a novel, and probably enough to finish this thing we'd started. Especially as long as Art was there seeing more in me than I saw in myself.

So aside from that one night, giving up was never really a consideration. Still, the tasks kept multiplying. Most of them intertwined and interdependent, requiring an organizational skill and, most importantly, a knowledge of the whole, a wide experience we simply didn't have.

Probably what saved us in the end was the fact that there was too much to do to think too much about how much there was to do. We kept managing to put our concentration into simply doing it, one hour at a time, one day at a time.

And I think also that neither of us wanted to let the other down. If Art was acting peevish or overwhelmed, I tended to play cheerleader sans pom poms until he got his equilibrium back. If I went silent or cranky, Art had a way of helping me see the bigger picture.

And lucky for me, he still does.

***

February, as usual, was shorter than January. The days were going the other way now, longer instead of shorter. But there was still snow and ice and wind.

I got to stay on top of the hill most of the time and deal with it there, but Art had to trot off to Boston every week and deal with it on the roads. Usually, that was an hour-and-a-half drive, and I could count on him to come walking up the hill (the driveway was usually too icy for driving most of that winter) by about five o'clock.

But one particular evening there was a terrific ice storm. I expected him to be late, but six o'clock came and went, then seven, then seven-thirty, then eight. I didn't expect him to be *that* late.

By eight-thirty I was convinced he was off the side of the road freezing to death in the woods or under a tractor-trailer on Rt. 395. Then, about quarter-to-nine, Lady raised her head off her paws and growled, listened, whimpered, jumped up with her tail wagging and went running down the path from the cabin.

I was right behind her, slipping and sliding all the way. Everything was covered with a coating of ice, and it was still coming down. The trees crackled. The footing was treacherous.

"Where on earth have you been?" I said, when I saw Art coming toward me. "I've been worried sick!"

He took my hand, shook his head. "If I tell you, you're probably not going to believe it."

We were driving a Honda Accord then. A car that had more history than some people I know. It was close to ten years old, and five teenagers had driven it. It had been in three accidents and had been totaled once, but it was all we had, and we weren't ready to put money into anything but the house for a while yet.

"Try me," I said, as we slid our way back to the cabin.

"The storm wasn't as bad in Massachusetts," Art started, "but once I got into Connecticut, the roads were slippery as hell. I couldn't go any faster than 20 miles an hour. Nobody was."

We got to the cabin, Art took off his ice-coated parka, and we sat down on the floor beside the kerosene heater. Ice hit the roof above us, sounding like a barrage of tiny metal balls. Even though it was freezing, I remember feeling almost cozy. And elated. Because he was here, he was okay.

"I was just past Auburn," he said, "and all of a sudden the car went totally out of control. I mean ... it was like some giant hand had taken control of the wheel and there I was, spinning around on the highway, and when I finally came to a stop, I was facing straight into oncoming traffic."

I had a sudden image of it, off headlights bearing down, horns blaring.

"My god, what did you *do*?"

"Waited for a break, turned the damn car around as fast as I could, and pulled into the breakdown lane." He shook his head. "I

Tima Smith

figured I'd blown a tire because there was no other reason for the car to skid like that ... I hadn't stepped on the brake, hadn't turned the wheel."

"And...?"

"All the tires were fine. So I got in and started driving again. And about five minutes later, it happened all over again!"

I looked at him. "You're kidding."

He shook his head. "It made no sense. The sanding trucks were out. Sure, everyone was going slow, but no one else was doing figure eights across the road. Just me. And this time the car went into the guard rail and took off the front bumper."

"You wrecked the car!?"

"Well, I wrecked the bumper."

We sat there for a second, not saying anything.

"So," he continued after a while, "I put the bumper in the trunk and started driving again."

"And it was okay after that."

"It happened two more times. I never went over five or ten miles an hour the rest of the way home."

The kerosene heater hissed, the ice continued pinging against the roof.

"Maybe we're being punished for leading really awful past lives," I said.

He sighed, shrugged. "Well, at least one good thing happened tonight."

I looked at him.

"I only fell twice walking up the driveway."

He looked at me. I looked at him. Then we started laughing. Maybe it was a kind of pathological hysteria, but whatever you want to call it, we laughed until it hurt too much to laugh anymore, while Lady dashed around, poking us with her nose as though she were trying to prod us back to being sane again.

We went to bed that night knowing we'd wake to an ice-encrusted world brilliant in the morning sun, and to an ice-encrusted Honda with a problem.

Luckily, in addition to house-builder, Art is the car mechanic around here. He had to wait a couple of days for the temperature to moderate and the ice to melt, and then he went down to the bottom of the hill with a box of tools and got under the Honda.

"Mystery solved," he said, when he finally reappeared.

"Poltergeists?" I asked.

"Close," he said. "One of the front brakes was locked."

"Which means...?"

"That one brake was on even when the brakes weren't on. A situation that tends to pull you in circles."

"So it's fixed," I said.

He started rummaging through a box of bolts. "Will be as soon as I reattach the bumper."

I watched him head back down the driveway. My own personal superhero.

Tima Smith

XI

 I found two part-time jobs and borrowed enough money from a friend to pay the reduced mortgage for a year. We were able to stay in the house while my three oldest finished high school in the town they'd grown up in.

 There was not a word from my ex. It was as if he'd disappeared into thin air. With, it turned out, every asset we owned – stocks, a life insurance policy. He even took my boat gear and my guitar. And of course there was no child support. But at least the divorce went through uncontested. All the hectoring and the invective stopped. In a strange way, his leaving made at least some things easier. But we weren't left totally alone. All that year, we received almost daily phone calls from someone who didn't speak, didn't hang up, just listened. There was no way to do a reverse look-up in those days, and, really, we didn't much care who it was ... just a daily five-second annoyance in a house where the phone seemed to ring constantly. Still, we were fairly certain it was Grandma. Listening to see who answered. Finding out if we were still there. Until finally my oldest daughter said into the phone, "we know it's you, Grandma. Why don't you say anything? Don't you want to talk to us?" After that, the calls stopped. It made me wonder who these people were; people I thought I'd known so well, but didn't really know at all. She'd come by once to ask my oldest daughter for a necklace she'd given her as a gift. She didn't get it.

 I realize she hated me. I could understand that. I'd made her son very unhappy. But he'd made me very unhappy, too. And why did hating me make her turn her back on her grandchildren? Especially at a time when they needed some constancy. Someone to talk to. Of course, she's long gone now, died alone from what I know. My ex had nothing to do with her after he disappeared. Her other son died soon after. Her whole family lost to her. All for no good reason.

CHAPTER SEVENTEEN

The Chimney

In March, the sun changed from a low silver disc in a gray sky to a somewhat higher yellow three-dimensional object that actually gave some degree of warmth if you raised your face to it.

The snow began to recede, and one weekend morning Greg and Brian showed up early. Brian went up on the roof with a snow shovel and off came the snow. Art applied the first row of tar paper and shingles, and by the end of the weekend, we had a roof.

They'd left the hole for the chimney, of course, plus a space in the peak directly behind the chimney big enough for a person to fit through. Access from the third floor made building the exterior part of the chimney much easier. And once the chimney was finished, someone would only have to make one trip up a ladder to close in that final hole. Someone who was not going to be me.

Now it was time to build it. The chimney. March, warm enough to work cement again.

The chimney consisted of an interior stack of tiles surrounded by a stack of cement chimney blocks. Chimneys are heavy things, so they need a footing that will support that weight and spread it over a larger area than the chimney's dimensions.

I decided I'd handle the chimney footing, because Art hated mixing cement. Besides, he was busy doing ten other things, and by the time he came by to check on what I was doing, the footing was done.

"What's that?" he said, pointing to my neat cement rectangle.

"It's the chimney footing," I said, "what do you think it is?"

He shook his head. I hated it when he shook his head like that.

"*That* can't support the chimney," he said, "it's too small."

"It is *not* too small."

"I'm telling you, Tima, it's too small. It should be twice that size."

I looked at it. "Okay," I said. "So I'll add to it."

"You can't *add* to it. It won't be tied together. All the weight will still be on this little piece of concrete!" He plunked a cement chimney block on top. "See?"

I'd banged together a form, dug out a one foot deep hole, mixed cement for half an hour in the wheelbarrow, made sure the top was smooth and flat. I hated being wrong. But he seemed so sure. And it *was* pretty small. Hardly larger than the chimney block.

We waited for it to harden a bit, dug it out, and carried it outside. Art built a new form to a size he was comfortable with and I did the cement thing all over again. The first footing became our front step for a while, until we built the mudroom. Then it got plunked at the edge of the lawn for a few years. Now it's a step for that third door we just put in on the northeast side of the house. When we build a deck outside *that* door, we'll leave the step where it is, which means it will disappear under the deck, and maybe I won't have to be reminded so often that I'm wrong a good deal of the time.

Reading about chimneys, we discovered they sway and require room to move as they pass through floors and through the roof. We also discovered they're somewhat mysterious, with no precise formula for achieving a good draft. So we simply assumed we'd get one and plowed ahead. The chimney tiles were light, no problem to carry and cement in place, but the cement blocks that surrounded them were another story, and they got mysteriously heavier and heavier the higher we went.

Jerry, our friend on the Cape, knew we were chimney-building and brought a friend up one day, a mason, to give us some tips. His name was Hoot and he didn't seem exactly thrilled to be spending a day in a cold skeleton of a house. He told us one thing and one thing only before he remembered he had to be somewhere else. And because of that one thing, I hope wherever he is today, he's having a really lousy time.

Our chimney was to be freestanding, unlike many that are built into the wall of a house, and he seemed to think stability was a problem. He told us to stuff cement between the tiles and the surrounding cement blocks as we went up in order to stiffen the structure.

Far as we knew, he was an expert, so we did what we were told. And then later, when we had to spend hours chipping the hardened cement out again, we made ourselves feel better by imagining him chained to the chimney, doing it all by himself with a pair of tweezers.

We had about eight feet of liner and block cemented when we decided to make the hole for the stove pipe before going any further. There was no reason to make the hole then, we just arbitrarily decided to do it, but we also decided to go and buy some pipe to make certain the hole was the proper size.

It was just one of those things that happens to work out for the best every once in a while.

The hardware store clerk was friendly and talkative and we just happened to mention what we were doing.

"Tricky," he said, "building a chimney. Sometimes they work and sometimes they don't."

"Well, we just want to make sure this one doesn't fall down," we said. And then we told him what we were doing, stuffing the space between the tile and the block with concrete.

"Oh jeeze," he said, "you don't want to do *that*."

"We don't?" we said.

Tima Smith

He shook his head. "Heck no. My father-in-law did that, too. No idea why. Soon as you start a fire and get those tiles hot, they're going to expand. What d'ya think's going to happen then?"

I wasn't sure, but I figured it was probably something bad.

"The tiles are going to crack," Art said.

So it *was* bad.

"My father-in-law," the clerk said, "had to rebuild his whole damn chimney."

Very *very* bad.

All the way home we talked about what might have happened if we'd waited to put the stove pipe in until the chimney was forty-feet of tile and cement block with no air space.

Because we'd only gone up eight feet, and because we could get some access from the stove pipe hole, which was at about six feet, we were able to chip out all the cement from the two feet in-between. We didn't worry about the area between the floor and the stove pipe because that part would never get hot.

Still, the chipping was tedious and difficult and very very slow. We spent almost two days on it. Two days we could have spent doing instead of undoing. Not to mention bleeding knuckles, cuts, scrapes, and all the curses we aimed at Hoot.

As soon as the channel between the tiles and the blocks was mostly clear of cement, we brought the chimney up to the first floor ceiling and cut the hole through. Michael E stopped by the next day on his way to someplace else, and even though he was in a hurry, he insisted on carrying the rest of the chimney blocks up to the second floor for us. There must have been twelve or thirteen of them, and because he was in a hurry and because he was late, what I remember is a blur of Michael running up and down the stairs, carrying each one of those heavy blocks and doing it in record time.

Oh yes. By then, we had a rough set of stairs to the second floor. Greg and a friend had built them one day when they got sick and tired of climbing the ladder. They put them up quickly, without any planning, so you had to step about two inches higher for the top two steps than the lower thirteen. But that staircase improved the quality of the workplace immeasurably. Of course, we should have had them sooner, but it only proved the mind-set that governed our project right from the beginning: If something worked, no matter how marginally (as in the ladder to the second floor) then you didn't take time to improve it. You put that time into something that wasn't working at all.

Art and I took the chimney all the way to the roof, and as far as I was concerned, that was far enough. Art had no problem going out on the roof. He'd been there through the raftering and the plywooding and the shingling. I, on the other hand, had tried to avoid even looking at it.

Because the chimney had to conform to a certain code, it had to be two feet taller than the tallest part of the roof ten feet away from it, which meant we had to add five feet to it from where it emerged through the roof.

I didn't want Art to have to do the chimney alone, so I took a deep breath and joined him. We began with him out on the roof and me going up and down the ladder carrying the tiles, which he cemented in place. For aesthetic reasons, we'd decided to switch from cement blocks to bricks above the roof, so I carried all those up, as well, and handed them to Art through the hole in the roof, along with a pail of cement.

Then, I tied one end of a rope around my waist, and had Art tie the other end to the tile chimney he'd just built. It was the only way I could function thirty-five feet above the ground on a sloping surface.

Neither of us had done any brickwork before, and building the chimney, carrying all those heavy materials up three levels, *and* being on the roof was already getting to me. All I wanted was for it to be over. So when Art suggested setting up strings to help keep the whole thing plumb and level, I balked.

Tima Smith

"We checked this cement block," I said, tapping the block that would be the base for the first layer of bricks. "It's perfectly level. If *it's* perfectly level, doesn't it make sense that anything on top of it will be perfectly level, too?"

He looked at me. For some reason he didn't argue. Maybe he decided his desire for precision was overkill this time. Plus, he could probably see I was just this side of sheer terror.

We started laying bricks. We eyeballed the whole thing, whipping the bricks up and around the tiles until we got to the top few layers. Then I took over the bricklaying while Art put on the lead flashing. Once we were done, I was down through the hole in the roof, down the ladder, down down down, never to return. Never.

Well ... at least that's what I thought at the time.

We went outside to the front yard to see how it looked. We stood there staring at it.

"Oh my God," I said.

"Hmmm," Art said.

"How did *that* happen?"

Art shook his head.

"How could it be so *completely crooked*??"

He shook his head again.

There was only one word for it ... ridiculous. There wasn't a straight corner or edge to be seen.

"Well," Art said, "maybe it doesn't matter."

"Doesn't matter!! *Doesn't matter*?? It looks like we did it blindfolded!"

"Well," Art said, "what are we going to do about it? Knock it down and do it over?"

Ah ... he'd hit me where it hurt.

Have I mentioned my extreme resistance to *redoing* things? More than a resistance, really. An unreasonable recalcitrance. Or maybe just a kind of lunacy. And he knew better than anyone that I'd do anything to avoid redoing something we'd put hours and hours into, or even minutes and minutes, only to spend hours and minutes doing it all over again.

"We are *not* taking that chimney down," I said.

"Okay, then we'll leave it. It's not that bad."

But it *was* that bad, and we both knew it. It was worse than bad. It was a disaster. We'd topped our house, a house that was turning out better than either of us had dared hope, with the most ridiculously crooked chimney anyone had ever built. It looked just a chimney in a cartoon.

"It's my fault," I said. "I'll fix it."

"How?" Art asked.

"I don't know, but I'll figure something out."

"Want me to help?" he asked.

I shook my head.

I had no idea how it could be fixed, or even *if* it could be fixed, but I did know one thing ... I wanted to fix it instantly. Before anyone came along and actually *saw* it.

I wish now that I'd taken a picture of it. But at the time it was the last thing in the world I wanted a reminder of.

***

Stones. It came to me the next day. For one thing, a stone chimney would be more attractive than brick. It would fit the setting, go better with the house. And for some reason, I had the idea it would fix the problem, make the chimney stop being crooked. I just wasn't sure why.

I walked around with the wheelbarrow, collecting a certain kind of stone. They had to be flat and of a certain thickness, definitely not too thick, but not too thin either. And they had to be a certain size. Bigger than my hand, but not much bigger, because I wanted to keep the weight down.

I mixed a very dry cement mix. The cement was going to have to hold these stones on a vertical surface, and I made my best guess at the ratio of cement to sand.

To his credit, Art hadn't even hinted at the fact that I'd been the one to shrug off the need for plumb and level lines. Plus, he seemed to realize how hard I'd taken this particular disaster. He offered to help once, but then left me alone to solve it myself. Not that there weren't enough other things to keep him busy. To keep twelve of him busy.

Or maybe he figured it would be good for me. To do this one thing that I hated more than anything else, to climb all the way out on that roof all by myself.

I made a dozen trips up and down the third floor ladder with my materials, set everything on the roof, and climbed through the hole holding on for dear life with one hand while I tied myself to the chimney with the other. For some reason, even tied to something as unmoving as that forty-foot chimney, I couldn't make myself work with both hands. I worked with one hand and held on to the chimney with the other. I simply couldn't help it.

The cement went on over the bricks, then I placed the stones. I didn't rush. I studied them, fitted them, they seemed to set well into the cement. The thing I was worried about was their staying there … through rain, snow, wind, and time.

It took me one entire afternoon, and when I was finished, I climbed down, called Art, and we walked to the front yard to see what, if anything, I'd accomplished.

"It looks grand," he said. "Good job!"

And he was right. The uneven stones had fully camouflaged the crooked lines of the bricks. It looked like a stone chimney. A straight, plumb, stone chimney.

Fifty Acres, More or Less

XII

In early spring, I put the house on the market. After it was sold, the money I walked away with – after paying utility liens, the mortgage, personal loans from friends, etc. – was enough, I figured, to last me three years if I was very very frugal. And that's exactly how long it lasted.

Just before we moved out of the house, I received a call from an insurance investigator. He wanted to question me about a deposition my ex had given in Florida several months earlier about an abandoned sailboat. Florida? Sailboat? Abandoned? The story left me speechless. According to the investigator, his insurance company was trying to locate my ex, who was wanted by the authorities in both Canada and Florida. Apparently, when he left for his 'two-weeks away', he went to Canada, where he stole and then launched the boat we'd been building. He broke into the building where it was stored, asked for and got the police to clear the way between the storage building and the wharf, launched the boat and sailed it to Florida. And did all of it using forged papers. He had been stopped by both the Canadian and American Coast Guards, but had talked his way out of both situations. He went along the inter-coastal waterway. There were others aboard, at least until he got to Florida. He insured the boat. Then sold everything on it -- except for one inflatable raft. He took the boat out into deep water, where, according to the investigator, the petcocks were opened and the boat was set adrift to sink. Except that it didn't sink. It only settled, because the petcocks became clogged with seaweed. A passing New York sailor salvaged the boat, which became his, according to the laws of salvage, after a period of time with no reply to newspaper notifications. The insurance company knew what my ex had done, or tried to do, and when he put in the claim for the insurance money on the basis that the boat had been stolen, they had him come in for a

Tima Smith

deposition. They asked him a hundred questions, all of which he handled brilliantly. When they asked him who he thought might want to steal the boat and sink it, the only person he could think of was me.

Of course, he never got the insurance money. Instead, the insurance company agents watched him leave the parking lot after the deposition and sent the police to his apartment to arrest him. But he never returned to his apartment. He knew he was in trouble, so he simply took his brand new white Cadillac, the one he'd paid cash for, and headed west. He had the rest of his life to justify it all.

CHAPTER EIGHTEEN

Floors

The next thing we had to do was get some flooring on the ground level so we could build interior walls and start on the wiring and plumbing. There weren't many walls on the first floor, just one between the kitchen and the bathroom, another between the bathroom and the utility room, and one to separate the utility room from the living room ell.

Both the brick for the kitchen, bathroom, and living room floors, and the natural stone for the utility room and the through-hallway were to go down on a mixture of dry cement and sand. Once the brick and stone were in place, we'd brush that same dry mix into the spaces and spray with water. This was supposed to be a good, quick floor.

It turned out to be neither particularly good, nor particularly quick. Although the reason for that was probably more due to *us*, our haphazard progression, than to a problem with the method. And actually, the kitchen and bathroom floors did turn out well. They were relatively small areas, easy to level, and the grout set properly and has remained hard. The brick floor in the living room was another story. As was the stone through-hallway.

After the chimney fiasco, we were sure to set level strings at floor height to insure the floors would be as straight and flat as people usually expect floors to be. And the kitchen and bathroom came out perfectly. The living room, however, which is the major part of the first floor, was too large to do in one session. In fact, it was months before it was completely finished.

Tima Smith

I started at one end of the living room and completed one 12x 15' area so we'd have a relatively clean place to set up a table for eating and working, and then stopped so I could work on things we needed more.

The rest of the floor, a good twenty feet in length, ended up being done piecemeal, most of it by visitors who seemed to think laying bricks was fun and easy. Often, I'd find several new rows of brick had been laid while I was off doing something else. The intention was helpful, yes, and when you compared it to other things we'd been doing, it was easy, maybe even fun. But unlike much of our work to that point, it required a serious degree of precision. The bricks needed to be spaced evenly and the surface should have been consistently level from one end of the room to the other.

It wasn't anyone's fault. I mean, how would they know that the level lines always needed to be reset. And what could you say? People were helping, volunteering, and doing it gladly. So eventually I just gave up. Besides, by then the floor had taken on a decidedly undulating character, and it became one of those things that we thought we'd redo once we had time. It still hasn't been redone.

To gather the stones for the hallway, we just had to walk outside. There were stones everywhere, perfect ones, flat and well-sized. And we chose them for their look, as well. Some are white mottled with black or gray, some are rust-colored, some bluish, some greenish, some gray, some black. We cleaned them and coated them with urethane before setting them in the dry mix, but they didn't go down nearly as easily or as quickly as the bricks.

For one thing, out of the three hundred stones we laid, there may have been ten that were flat both on the top *and* the bottom. The other 290 had to be settled-in according to their bottom surface. And then after all that work, the walking surface wasn't nearly as even as a floor should be.

Fifty Acres, More or Less

Because the bottoms of the stones were uneven, and because they were set into a thin, dry mix, they tended to move when they were walked on. This broke the grouting and made a general mess.

We lived with them for about five years and then when I couldn't stand it anymore, I took them up in sections, swept away the dry grout, and bedded them in concrete. The way we should have laid them in the first place.

I treat both the bricks and the stones every two years or so with a protective masonry coating. It provides a sheen and brings out the colors in the stones.

The floors seem to do a fine job as a heat sink, though they're absolutely unforgiving if you drop a glass. For a while, I did feel the hardness in my legs, but then I seemed to get used to it. A rug in front of the sink helps. The plastic sheeting and the rigid insulation beneath must be working, because the floors have never conducted dampness even under the wettest conditions. And they're not especially cold in the winter.

***

Once most of the floor was down, we were able to put up the interior first floor walls and start the wiring and plumbing. By then, it was the end of March. The temperatures at night were still in the thirties, but with walls around the utility room we were able to plug in a heater and leave it running at night so the water in the pressure tank wouldn't freeze. Until then, we'd only had water when it became absolutely necessary. Now, we could have water anytime. Cold water, yes, but water whenever we needed it.

As far as cleanliness went that winter, we were on a catch-as-catch-can kind of schedule. Art got his hot showers when he drove into Boston and stayed overnight. Lauren had daily access to showers at the gym in school, and in a pinch, in the tiny shower in her trailer, although it delivered very little water and never heated it to more than lukewarm.

I had to drive to Jen's dorm to take a shower, and that often took too much energy to do it with any regularity.

Tima Smith

What I discovered is that after the first three days, it's amazingly easy to adjust to being dirty. Although I do remember standing in line at a supermarket in my grungy work clothes once, and catching a reflection of myself that shocked me. Refugees I'd seen on TV looked better. And I had to wonder … did they smell better, too?

Lauren and I would spend an hour or two in the evenings talking, and our conversations always ended with a slew of wishful thinking.

As soon as we have hot water, I'm going to take the longest shower in the history of the world. (Lauren)

When we have a refrigerator again, I'm going to fill it with so much food the door won't close. (me)

I'm going to have a huge party. (Lauren, and she did.)

I'm going to bake some bread, because I haven't smelled that smell in so long I can't remember it anymore. (me)

And finally, Lauren: *I'm never going near another trailer as long as I live.*

***

If we were going to have any luck at all, April was going to usher in warmer, longer days, the promise of spring and summer, an end to being cold and mostly miserable. We inched forward, automatons who got up at dawn and worked late every night, or at least until we stopped making good decisions.

Then Art and I trudged off into the woods to our cabin, where we sat on the floor in our heavy coats next to the kerosene heater. Art read his students' work, I wrote stories. When we couldn't keep our eyes open any longer, we crawled under our fourteen blankets and went to sleep, then got up at dawn and did the same thing all over again.

CHAPTER NINETEEN

Wiring and Plumbing

Once the interior walls were up, I got started on providing the basics for water and power. By then we had plywood kitchen counters that finally gave us someplace to put things besides the floor or the stairs or the folding chairs we carried around from workstation to workstation.

Having places to *put* things is an amazingly civilized accomplishment. For a very long time, that lack of simple order caused its own mental and physical chaos.

There was something about keeping everything on the floor that was strangely disorienting. I'm sure that early man must have evolved several notches the first time someone placed a stone tool in a niche on the cave wall.

Order is, quite simply, a very comforting state, and the counters provided that comfort. All of a sudden, tools had a specific place, and we spent much less time hunting for them. Spreading a paper towel created a clean spot to make a peanut butter and jelly sandwich. Heaven.

Greg came one day, and because the extension ladder we'd used for climbing to the third floor was outside being used for the exterior siding, he banged together a wall ladder to the third floor. We ended up using it far too long, but it made getting to the third floor a whole lot easier.

Stairs, counters, floors, walls. The place was almost starting to feel homey.

***

Tima Smith

The plumbing was relatively simple. It was contained, more or less, on one wall. Water entered under pressure, exited thanks to gravity. It was an easy concept to visualize.

Electricity, on the other hand, was more complex. It flowed, too, like water, but you had to figure out how to control that flow with switches and junctures. You had to plan branches. You had to know when to switch to three wire Romex and how to wire differently for a switch *before* a light fixture than a switch *after* a light fixture. And you had to drill at least five hundred holes. Well, maybe not *five* hundred. But close.

I learned that with two-wire Romex (which actually includes a third copper wire for grounding), the black wire is hot and the white wire is neutral, except under certain circumstances — for instance three-way switches or a light in the middle of a circuit ... when the white wire becomes hot, as well, and needs to be marked black to show that.

I discovered the reason for three-wire Romex, which has a copper grounding wire, a white neutral, and two hot wires — a black and a red. Using it where a light at the end of the circuit is controlled by a pair of three-way switches, you need a third hot wire, and, once again, the white neutral wire becomes hot and must be so marked.

Get the idea?

Well, maybe it sounds all a-jumble, but what I discovered is that you can do something without absolutely understanding why you're doing it. For $5.95, I bought a Sunset book entitled *Basic Home Wiring Illustrated* and followed it almost exclusively. It had clear, well-identified illustrations and simple explanations. Everything I needed was in it except for one thing — three switches controlling one light. Eventually, I figured that one out for myself.

The first thing I'd done when I stated planning for the wiring was to walk through the house, imagining where I'd want switches and overhead lighting. I wanted to be able to walk from one area to another turning on a light as I entered and turning it off as I left. The idea was to never retrace my steps to turn off a light. In general, I knew what the electric code called for. Separate small appliance 20-amp branch circuits for the kitchen and the laundry and the dishwasher. Separate 50 amp circuits for the stovetop and oven and hot water heater. A 30-amp 120/240 major appliance circuit for the electric dryer. Outlets spaced not more than twelve feet apart.

I divided 500 into the total square footage to get a rough idea of how many 15-amp circuits to create for the rest of the house, erring on the side of too many rather than too few. I planned conservatively the number of outlets and switches for each circuit. And as far as spacing the outlets was concerned, I added more wherever it seemed like a good idea, so today, no matter where you want to plug something in, there's a place to do that.

I planned for ground fault outlets near sinks in the bathroom and kitchen and outdoors. Plus, I planned for future add-ons, as well — for the garage we planned to build some day, and the porch, and the deck. And there was exterior lighting: outside fixtures near doors, and flood lights for the front, back, and side yards.

It was a well-researched, thoughtful plan. Especially for someone who'd never heard of a single-pole switch or used a wire stripper. I knew, as I drew a diagram of all the potential outlets and switches, that I still had a lot to learn. But learn I did.

The first step was hanging a circuit breaker box in the utility room. All the wiring started from there. Because we had no basement, there were no short cuts for running the wiring. The wiring for outlets on the south wall, the wall directly opposite the circuit breaker box, had to start at the box on the north wall and run through the north wall, the east (or west) wall and then through the south wall to the outlet. For the outlets farthest from the breaker box, that was a distance of approximately sixty-five feet.

If we had a house with a basement, we would have installed the circuit breaker box there and run the wiring across the basement ceiling and then directly up through the wall to the outlets. We probably used triple the amount of Romex doing it our way.

The second floor had the same problem, and the third. Most houses have ceilings constructed of 2x4 stringers with the floor above attached to the tops of the stringers and the ceiling of the room below attached to the bottoms. That leaves a space between the stringers to run wires.

But our ceilings were different. The first floor ceiling was the bottom layer of a three-layer sandwich. The top layer of the sandwich was the tongue and groove floor of the bedrooms above. No space for wiring. On the second floor, the two front bedrooms have cathedral ceilings where wires could be run. But the rear of the second floor (a third bedroom, a laundry area, a full bath, and a sitting room) had the third floor above, with the same sort of ceiling/floor construction as the first floor.

In other words, there were very few shortcuts for the wiring, and, aside from the walls, very few places to hide them.

I must easily have drilled two hundred holes. Because of the combination stick/post & beam construction, some of these holes had to go through laminated beams six and seven-and-a-half inches thick. I chose a Forstner drill bit after trying a few others and never had a problem. The Forstner never caught or jammed, never made the drill twist in my hands, never knocked me off my ladder. Not once.

Much later, after the bulk of the electric work was long over, I was watching a segment of *This Old House.* Steve and Norm were visiting a tool show. They stopped to look at a new tool specifically designed to drill holes for wiring. Norm picked it up and commented on what a good idea it was. He called it a great improvement over the 'wrist breakers' and 'widow makers' that were normally used.

Fifty Acres, More or Less

Since watching that show, I've done four or five wiring additions, and every time, *every single time*, the drill bit has caught in the wood. Once, on my knees, the handle of the drill spun and caught me in the jaw and almost knocked me out. The other three times, the bit has caught and twisted hard enough to pull the drill out of my hands. It has to make you wonder … that I only encountered problems *after* I learned how dangerous drilling could be.

It took about a month to drill all the holes, pull hundreds of feet of wire, and install the boxes (we used plastic) for all the switches, outlets, and fixtures throughout the entire house.

Then as soon as that was done, I started on the plumbing. The building inspector needed to inspect both the rough wiring and the rough plumbing and I wanted him to be able to do that in one visit.

So far, the building inspector had been pleasant and easy to work with, but he'd only come once, to okay the depth of the foundation. When he came to inspect the electric and plumbing, he'd look at the structure, as well, and we tried not to think too much about what his reaction was going to be.

Because one bathroom was directly above the other and both of them, along with the kitchen and laundry, were on the north wall, the plumbing was a fairly compact installation. We'd decided to use CPVC plastic for everything. CPVC is approved for hot water lines as well as cold, and when we did our research, we could find no evidence that copper was worth the extra expense and trouble. So far, the CPVC has been durable and trouble-free, and it was certainly easier for an amateur installation.

I used Genova pipe and fittings for the incoming pressurized system. All I needed to do was measure accurately and glue it together. Within seconds of gluing, the joint was absolutely immovable, so you had to make sure you did it right the first time. But even if you didn't, you could always cut your mistake off and glue on another piece the right way. The Genova instruction manual claimed that after 24 hours a pipe would burst before a joint failed, and I believe that.

The outgoing waste system called for more planning, mainly because of venting, which prevents sewage gas from invading the house, and also because the horizontal pipes have to have a gentle pitch to let gravity take over. These pipes were from 1 1/2" to 3" in diameter, and rigid, which meant they were much less forgiving to work with than the 1/2" water pipe, which had some give to it.

Traps (those s-shaped things under sinks and other appliances) are always filled with water, which keeps sewer gases within the pipes from roaring up through the sink drain. If installed improperly, a waste system can cause that water to drain, letting vapor rise up the pipe. This all has something to do with the proximity of the vent stack (that pipe coming out of the roof that releases sewer/septic tank gases where no one will notice) to the various plumbing fixtures.

By code, all fixtures need to be within a certain number of feet from the vent stack. Our kitchen sink did not comply. It was too far away by several feet, and I knew that the best way to handle that was a second vent pipe specifically for that sink which would feed into the main stack at a point higher than the highest fixture in the house.

But I didn't want to run a second stack. It would have meant a second set of holes to drill (and these weren't small holes like wiring holes or water pipe holes, these were huge!) and I was rapidly getting sick to death of drilling holes. So I decided to handle it a different way and hope for the best.

***

Once the wiring and plumbing were roughed in, we called the building inspector and he came out promptly. He seemed interested in the whole house, and took his time inspecting everything. When he was done, he said, "Well you certainly did

Fifty Acres, More or Less

overbuild. This place is never coming down." Then he added, "You've done a good job."

We felt a huge sense of relief. But it wasn't over yet.

He approved the wiring without a problem, but suggested having an electrician look it over once the final wiring was completed. I told him we planned to have an electrician transfer the electricity from the temporary hookup to the circuit breaker box and that we'd ask him to check the wiring then.

The last thing he looked at was the plumbing. Everything was fine until he got to that pesky kitchen sink. He squatted in front of it, studying the pipes, and I knew what he was thinking and I knew what he was going to say.

Then he said it. "This fixture's too far from the main stack."

"Yes, I know," I said. "That's why I used oversized pipe, 2" instead of 1 1/2", so there'll be room for vapor and waste at the same time."

He stared at it some more. I held my breath.

Finally, he nodded. "I think that's right," he said, "that should work. If you do notice an odor, though, you'll have to add a stack."

But there's been no odor. No second stack.

***

Once it had all been approved, I threw myself into wiring up all the switches and lights and outlets, a cinch compared to drilling holes and pulling wire. Mechanical, repetitive, almost meditative. There were roughly 150 connections, including switches, outlets, lights, a third-floor fan.

All the wires left the circuit breaker box neatly. They were properly grounded, properly connected to the hot bus bars and the neutral bus bar. Of course none of it could be tested because the circuit breaker box itself wasn't hooked up yet, and the closer we came to that, the more nervous I got. Would it all work? Would *any* of it work? And if it didn't, would I be able to figure out why?

Tima Smith

***

While I'd been working on the electricity and the plumbing, Art had been installing the rest of the windows, building counters in the bathrooms, putting up cupboards and shelves in the kitchen, and building a beautiful cedar-walled shower in the upstairs bathroom. We went out and bought a stainless steel double sink for the kitchen and installed it, toilets, a downstairs bathroom sink, a hot water heater. Hot water? I didn't dare to believe it. We bought a used double-oven and a refrigerator.

It was all terrific.

And then it was May. No more freezing nights. No more fifteen blankets.

Two electricians came to power up the circuit breaker box and hook up the oven and the counter top range. The cable for those two appliances was gigantic, stiff and difficult to work, and by then I felt I deserved that much of a break. While one electrician was wiring the oven, he asked me who did all the wiring. I told him I'd done it, and he laughed.

"No really," I said, "I did it myself."

He came out from under the counter and looked at me. "The whole house?"

I nodded.

"How did you know how?" he asked. "Did you go to school?"

"I read a book," I told him.

He looked at me for a second. "Jeeze," he said, and disappeared back under the counter.

The electricians seemed to catch our anticipation, and our anxiety, and as soon as they were done, as soon as the main switch was thrown on, we all gathered in the kitchen.

"Go ahead," one of them said, "try a light."

I shook my head. "I can't."

So he flipped the light switch himself. The overhead light came on. "It works!" he said, and grinned at me.

Fifty Acres, More or Less

We were all grinning. We tried a few more. They worked, too.

I felt like I'd created the world.

Within the course of one morning, we went from one outlet and five extension cords to power everywhere.

"I can't believe I actually did it," I told Art.

He looked at me. "Anyone who could straighten that chimney can do anything."

I went through the entire house, and, one by one, flipped every switch, tried every outlet. They worked ... all of them! Lights went on, lights went off. Radios played. The water in the hot water tank got hot.

I knew exactly how Thomas Edison must have felt.

And the plumbing, that worked, too. The toilets flushed. No more outhouse! Faucets ran hot and cold. Sinks drained. After a year without running water, we had a washing machine *and* a shower! Suddenly cleanliness was back in our lives. And for a very long time, switching on a light or plugging in the vacuum or turning on the shower was no unconscious act. They were all small miracles. And when you really stop and think about, that is what they are. Miracles.

Tima Smith

CHAPTER TWENTY

Moving In

Even though the house was still open at the eaves and the second-floor interior walls only consisted of studs, Lauren couldn't wait. She moved into her bedroom lock, stock, and barrel. She'd had more than enough of that tiny, dark trailer, the cramped bunk, the mice. And who could blame her?

We carried the parts of her double bed from the cabin and set it up. Then she spent the day plowing through boxes, reclaiming everything she'd packed away a year earlier. We hung a rod in her big see-through closet so she could finally hang up her clothes.

Posters surfaced, a full-length mirror, a very large radio, a white trim–line phone.

How she'd stood that year so uncomplainingly, I'll never know. I'll just be eternally grateful to her for being as mature about the experience as you could expect any sixteen-year-old to be. When I think about it, I realize we don't talk about that time, Lauren and I. I suppose it's because we'd both like to forget how hard and unforgiving and desolate it all too often seemed.

But moving into her room made everything much much better.

And it was too much of a good idea not to follow suit. So, about two weeks later, Art and I installed sheetrock on the closet walls between Lauren's room and ours, and then moved in ourselves.

We had nothing but bare rafters above our heads, stud walls all around. Sometimes Lauren and I talked to each when we were in bed at night without even raising our voices.

Fifty Acres, More or Less

And now, when I look back, it seems that moving in should have been done with at least a degree of fanfare. But all we did was set up our bed and climb the stairs that night instead of tramping off through the woods to the cabin.

I think, by that time, we were numb to celebration or euphoria or glee. We'd been existing for so long on a treadmill, we couldn't have stopped to smell a rose if we'd wanted to. Steve, the young man who'd rolled over in the Case, had presented us with a bottle of champagne before he left.

"To open when the house is done," he'd said. But 'done' was a concept we'd lost somewhere along the way.

Still, something occurred early the morning after we moved in that I'll always remember. It woke me out of a sound sleep, and I lay there listening for a while, half-awake, until it hit me that it sounded like something impossible. Like the sound of a dragon breathing. I opened my eyes.

Inhale, exhale, inhale, exhale. A huge rasping noise that grew louder and louder. What on earth...? And then through the window, a hot air balloon floated into sight. It was a vivid explosion of red, purple, blue, and yellow in the rising sun, the heater firing and dying, firing and dying. It was close enough to clearly see two people in the gondola, and I woke Art.

"Listen," I said.

He did, and then he frowned, and when I pointed, he looked toward the window.

We got up and watched until it was gone. A lovely site to wake up to. And, perhaps, celebration enough.

But just to officially mark the occasion, Jennifer came that first weekend with a boyfriend, a bottle of wine, and a picnic. Checkered tablecloth and all.

Tima Smith

CHAPTER TWENTY-ONE

LADY

We decided to have a party in May, and invited everyone we knew who'd been hearing stories about our project and were intensely curious to see what it was all about.

We had warned everyone not to wear good clothes, and held the party upstairs on the second floor because much of the floor in the living room was still dirt. We also warned each person going up the stairs to "watch those two top steps, because they're higher than the others!" Even though our friend Nick had scribbled a message on one of the step risers – *Please fix me!* (and eventually, we did).

Lady, our Black Lab, was at the party, too. She went from person to person looking for a little attention and a handout. She'd developed mammary cancer, and we didn't know how much time she had left, but she was enjoying herself that spring, with a new house to protect. She was close to fifteen, gray in the muzzle. She'd been our constant companion, roughing it when we roughed it, following along after the Case, walking the utility trench, barking at the cement truck, lying at a respectful distance while we cut trees, always protective, hardly ever more than a few feet away.

Some time after the party was over and everyone was gone, I happened to be looking out the window when she tried to jump over a stone wall. She missed, and fell hard against the stones. I knew she'd hurt herself.

That night, she climbed up onto my side of the bed, something she hadn't done since she was a puppy. She was breathing hard, in

Fifty Acres, More or Less

pain, and she stayed there beside me all night, moaning. None of us got any sleep.

Early the next morning, I called our vet, Betty Norris. Betty had started her practice in Pomfret about the time we'd moved here. She was right down the street, and she'd already treated Lady, so she knew exactly what was happening.

By then, Lady was in so much pain, I didn't want to move her, and I asked Betty if she could come. She didn't hesitate, only asked that someone meet her at the bottom of the hill so she wouldn't have to drive up.

Art carried Lady downstairs because we knew she needed to go outside, and somehow she managed to pee, then he brought her into the living room and lay her on a blanket. Betty took one look and said it was time. There was no argument from me or from Art. By then, Lady was rigid with pain and we both just wanted it to be over for her. In seconds, it was. She sighed, relaxed, and then she was gone.

After Betty left, Art and I wrapped Lady in a blanket and carried her to a spot a little way down the hill on the east side of the house. In my mind, I kept seeing her in snapshot images — a four-week-old puppy scratching at my ankles to be picked up, watching me with big soulful eyes whenever she had to stay behind, slinking sheepishly back into the tent the night of the skunk, being protective against strangers we'd meet walking along the abandoned railroad bed. We cried the whole time we were burying her.

She left a big empty space on the hill and we mourned her and missed her for a very long time.

Tima Smith

CHAPTER TWENTY-TWO

Finally, Walls!!

So much had been done, and yet there was still so much to do.

We were living in a house under construction, which meant in a way we were still camping out, except now we were doing it with the addition of sawdust. The table saw was in the living room, along with a circular saw and our supply of lumber. The living room floor was still dirt, every surface rough wood, most of the walls still studs. Inside, we needed closets, insulation, a third-floor floor and a second-floor ceiling, and we needed to start the finish work — tile counters in the kitchen and bathrooms, doors, the rest of the living room's brick floor.

Brian was moving back home after his freshman year at college, so more than anything we needed walls, especially interior bedroom walls.

This was about the time we discovered the sixteen-foot wood trimmings bundled behind the lumber yard woodshed at the bottom of our hill. Owner Bill Lambot had urged us many times to take what we wanted. "Even if you just use it for kindling," he said, "it's good dry wood, and we can't give it away."

It was northwest pine and aspen trimmings that contained imperfections which made it unsalable as trim woodwork, but it was clear (no knots) and the 'imperfections' were simply off-shadings, which we quite liked. Yes, each board was only two inches wide, which meant four of these were necessary to cover the same width as one eight-inch wide shiplap or tongue and groove board. Which meant a lot of extra nailing and extra time. But each board was sixteen-feet long. They'd cover any wall in one full strip with no piecing. The question was … how would they look?

I was pushing to get the washer and dryer in place because now that our clothes were once again accessible, cleaning them had moved way up on the priority list. The laundry backed against the second floor bathroom, and although we'd fallen into a sort of polite dance of avoiding the open-walled bathrooms when they were occupied, finishing that wall between the toilet and the laundry seemed like a really really good idea. Plus, since it wasn't going to be particularly noticeable, I decided it was an excellent candidate for an experiment with all that free wood sitting down at the bottom of the hill.

After it was finished, we stood back and studied it.

I'd staggered the wood so that half of the pine strips were horizontal and the other half vertical.

Conclusion: It looked great.

Bill's piles of trimmings shrank as we finished most of the second floor walls and much of the first. We considered using his wood for the cathedral ceilings in the bedrooms, too, although we did wonder if it might be too much of a good thing. Should we or shouldn't we? We couldn't decide. And since the ceilings were still un-insulated, and there were four months of summer ahead, we decided to put the ceilings off for a while.

In hindsight, it was probably for the best, but by the time we decided to use the free wood, it wasn't free anymore ... or rather, it simply wasn't *there* anymore. While we procrastinated during the summer and into the fall, the economy began to sour, especially the building trades, and Lambot Lumber was forced into thriftiness. Cutting off two inches of a board and consigning it to the garbage heap had become a thing of the past.

The ceilings would wait a decade before they were finished, during which time there was always something to read when you were lying in bed staring at the ceiling ... *Owens-Corning Fiberglas Building Insulation Assured Thermal Performance R-30. Warning: The Facing On This Insulation Will Burn And Should NOT Be Left Exposed.*

Tima Smith

***

June, glorious June. But now that the weather was warm again, the open eaves were a problem. They let everything in — birds, bugs, bats, bees.

Somebody had to enclose them, and since they were well above my eighteen-foot ladder limit, it wasn't going to be me. It was all up to Art, and anybody else who dared.

Our twenty-four-foot extension ladder wasn't nearly tall enough to reach even close to the roof at the gable ends or the rear wall, but Art was fearless when it came to heights. Plus, he had a plan.

He drove the Case right up to the wall, the bucket facing it, then set the bottom of the ladder in the bucket and raised the bucket as high as necessary. He claims the ladder was safer there than on the ground, but you couldn't prove it by me. It looked as though you had to be insane to trust it.

Safe or not, insane or not, Art worked on the eaves and the highest siding. But it went very very slowly. It took forever to position the Case, position the ladder, climb up and do the narrow section within arm's reach, then climb down and do it all over again.

"You need staging," Greg announced.

"It's too expensive to rent," Art said.

"No problem," Greg said. "We can build it ourselves. All we need are 2x4s and planking." Those words still echo in my ears. And probably in Brian's, too.

So they built their own staging. If that's what you want to call it. To be accurate, it was more like an *approximation* of staging. A *facsimile*. A very very distant cousin. And the only two words I could use to describe it were *absurdly dangerous*. And I wasn't the only one. To this day, if you ask Greg or Art or Brian what the most dangerous part of the entire house building project was, they'll say, "That staging!"

Of course, Greg wouldn't admit it at the time, since it was his idea and he directed how to build it, but today he says it's a miracle it didn't collapse and that someone didn't die. There were only three uprights across a thirty-six-foot span, which meant that the twelve-inch wide planks that people stood on bowed dangerously under their weight. Especially when two people were standing on the same section. The only good thing about it is that the work got done very very fast because no one wanted to be out there any longer than they absolutely had to be.

As it turned out, the eaves were done a little *too* quickly. They were enclosed, but never really *finished*. There was no trim, for instance, to cover small spaces and chinks. These were spaces and chinks that none of us particularly noticed back then, but they were spaces and chinks that were to become highly visible the following fall to every kind of critter that was looking for a nice warm, dry home for the winter.

Tima Smith

CHAPTER TWENTY-THREE

Critters

We were inundated.

I have no idea why it didn't occur to us that the cabin we spent that awful winter in was full of mice. I mean, didn't we see them scurrying here and there? Didn't we hear them? It makes perfect sense that since the old shot-up trailer was full of mice, and Lauren's trailer was full of mice, that the cabin would be full of mice, too. All of Pomfret is full of mice!

But it was dark in that cabin. Hard to see one's hand, never mind a tiny little lurking mouse. And when we went to sleep, we were so exhausted, a mouse could have run straight across my face and then straight across Art's, and probably neither of us would have noticed.

When we moved into the house, of course, we brought in all our boxes from the cabin … clothing, non-perishable food, books. I realize now there were probably mice in those boxes, and we simply carried them all right on into the house.

They were thrilled. They multiplied.

For a long time, we had lots of company at night. Mice running along the ceiling beams, mice peeking out from behind the insulation, mice gnawing, mice scratching, mice squeaking, mice running across the floor and making you jump just when you'd settled down at the end of the day.

For a while, we felt a certain sense of tolerance for them. They were tiny, they were scared, and some of them, especially the gray ones with big ears, were cute. We bought a have-a-heart trap and set it every night, using peanut butter as bait. And every night, often several times a night, we'd hear its little tin doors bang shut and either Art or I would carry the trap some distance from the house and release the mouse.

This is when we discovered that mice have unique personalities. Some cowered in the trap. Some ran back and forth, jumping at the wire mesh. Others just sat and looked at us. Some would bound straight out of the trap as soon as you opened the door. Others would sniff and proceed with caution. And some wouldn't come out of the trap no matter what. As far as they were concerned the devil they knew was preferable to the devil they didn't. And who could blame them? Why would they want to trade a bed of warm pink insulation for a cold, dark brush pile.

But after a while, all the mice, regardless of personality, seemed to be getting pretty comfortable with the have-a-heart routine. They didn't seem particularly afraid of us, ran straight out of the trap as soon as we opened the door, and no matter how many we caught and took outside, the number of mice in the house never seemed to diminish.

It finally dawned on us that as far as the mice were concerned, we were all involved in some bizarre, but highly acceptable, feeding ritual. We fed them peanut butter, jars and jars of it. For some reason they could probably never figure out, we then carried them outside and let them go. And then, they just hurried straight back into the house to do it all over again.

Okay. So they were getting back in. But how?

We had it in our minds that mice were burrowers, not climbers. But as we walked around the house, we noticed scratch marks all the way up one front corner straight into a tiny space in the eave.

We blocked it. But by then, the mice population was impossible, and we were feeling decidedly less empathetic toward them. Especially after I decided to change the location of a light switch one day and discovered that the wire had been chewed almost through.

Okay, I decided, looking at that wire. This was war.

Tima Smith

The have-a-heart went on the shelf in favor of One-Bite rat poison. It took five boxes. Ten bags per box. That's a lot of poison. But then, there were a LOT of mice.

***

The flying squirrels came later, after the house was more finished.

They were quite large, as rodents go. And peculiarly unafraid of us. Because they were nocturnal, they had very large eyes. And they seemed to enjoy staring at you with them. As far as I could see, they didn't blink. And if they happened to be clinging high on a wall, they were apt to leap off with all four limbs spread and hang-glide just inches over your head.

The first time I saw one, I was at the computer on the third floor. I happened to look across the room and swore I saw something clinging to my brand new ficus plant. Then it leaped onto the wall above the window and hung there watching me.

To get to the stairs, I had to cross right in front of it, and for a good ten minutes or so, I didn't know what was worse, sitting there with this unpredictable creature staring at me from a distance, or narrowing our proximity so that I could run downstairs and escape. Finally, I yelled for Art, who put himself between me and the thing until I was downstairs.

As far as the flying squirrels were concerned, they'd found a very big cave to live in for the winter. Sure, it was a cave inhabited by other creatures that were much larger and a lot noisier, but that didn't seem to bother them at all. We found out very quickly that nothing minor was going to make them leave. Plus, they didn't want just a small portion of the cave, they wanted the whole second and third floors.

Blame the scaffolding.

The flying squirrels were climbing the house and coming in through the eaves. Eaves that were never sealed because no one wanted to stay on the scaffolding long enough to really finish the job.

We didn't know until we removed the insulation from the roof just above the top of the third floor wall and looked into those eaves just how poorly they'd been boxed in. We didn't find narrow cracks, we found spaces large enough for a small cat to squeeze through. It explained why the third floor was so cold in the winter, especially on a windy day. And it explained the flying squirrels.

Problem: They were active only at night. During the day they were fast asleep in our eaves. Working on the eaves from the outside during the day would drive them *into* the house or possibly into whoever was out there on the ladder, and we definitely didn't want either of those things.

Solution: Because we still didn't have finished interior walls on the third floor, we could work on the eaves from the *inside*. But no one was particularly anxious to do that while the squirrels were present during the day.

But then we discovered we could dislodge them by making a huge racket. Hammering from the inside on the wood surrounding their nests got them out of the eaves, onto the outer walls, got them leaping into the air, gliding to the ground, and running into the woods. Where they should have been in the first place.

We stationed Michael outside to yell up and tell us what he saw once we started hammering. "They're coming out!" he yelled. "Oh shit, there's a hundred of 'em." Well, maybe he was exaggerating.

While they were temporarily evicted, we removed all the insulation from the ceiling near the eave, cleaned out the eave box (don't ask what was in there), sprinkled in a good supply of moth balls (we'd heard that might help discourage them), and tacked up wire mesh so even if they *did* get back into the eaves, at least they couldn't get into the house.

We had to use wire mesh instead of solid wood because the eaves are part of the roof ventilation system. The roof of our house is so heavily insulated, there's a possibility of roof rot from vapor

Tima Smith

condensation on the underside of the plywood. To avoid this problem, we'd installed a ridge vent along the peak of the roof, and rigid foam channels between the rafters to allow air to circulate. Presumably, air enters through a vent strip in the eaves, flows up the roof along the foam channels, and then out the vent at the peak.

Once the wire mesh was installed, we borrowed a bucket truck (highly recommended over a ladder) and Michael volunteered to go up and properly seal the eaves on the outside, as well.

The squirrels weren't happy. We heard them running on the sides of the house, up, down, back and forth, trying to find ways in for days. We gave them a hard time by shining lights at them and making a lot of noise. Finally they gave up and went off in search of a new home.

Once again we had the cave all to ourselves.

Bats were never a big problem, although we had them nesting up under the roof until we finally finished the trim work on the gable ends and eliminated the spaces they were using as an entry. We would never have known they were there except for the young bats, who often got confused about which direction was *out* at dusk. Every spring, we'd have at least one bat flying around inside the house until we opened a window and it managed to find its way out.

CHAPTER TWENTY-FOUR

A Slow Summer, Another Cold Winter

Our first summer in the house felt like a luxury. It was warm inside, warm outside. We were no longer in a frantic rush. The worst was over.

We had an old Better n' Ben's sheet metal stove to hook up to the chimney, and before the end of May, before it got too hot and buggy to be doing such hard work outside, we split and stacked about six cords of firewood.

We built closets, finished a storage area on the third floor, put in book shelves and a big wooden countertop with storage underneath to divide the kitchen from the entry hall.

I found a part-time job at the University of Connecticut and sold some stories. Lauren got accepted at a Connecticut college and went to her senior prom. Brian and Michael came home for the summer. In general, things began to feel as though they were under some degree of control.

And then Art almost sliced off his thumb.

I was outside cleaning windows and Art was inside using the table saw. I heard him yell, looked through the glass and saw him holding his hand. Then I saw blood. I rushed inside.

"It's pretty bad," he said. "What a damned stupid thing to do."

I looked at his hand just long enough to know that at least his thumb was still mostly attached, then we wrapped it in a towel and took off for the emergency room.

It was a very deep cut, right to the bone, and it ended up putting him out of commission far longer than it should have. After four weeks, the wound had to be reopened because it was healing improperly. The pain was terrible. It was the only time I'd ever known Art to resort to pain killers. And even after the thumb healed, it was overly sensitive to cold, heat, and pressure for a long time.

Work slowed to a crawl, which wasn't entirely a bad thing. We'd been slaving without a break for over a year by then, doing hard physical work, and we needed to slow down.

I turned my attention to outdoor work, cleaning up the piles of debris that were everywhere in the yard. We bought a brush-trimmer and grass seed. We sold Lauren's trailer. We ate real meals every evening, watched TV at night, discovered the student theater at the University of Connecticut. In other words, we started living like normal people doing normal things.

I think we were under the impression that summer would go on forever.

But of course it didn't.

Suddenly it was Labor Day, Brian and Michael were going back to college, Lauren was starting her freshman year. Where had the summer gone? Art's thumb was still sensitive to pressure, and I think we were still in recovery from the constant push. Leaves started to fall. It got cold.

It was going to be our first winter in the house, but we weren't worried. We had the Better n' Ben's and a good supply of dry firewood. And after last year's winter, anything had to be an improvement, didn't it?

Yes, of course it did. But we ended up discovering all sorts of things that winter. That the house was far from air-tight. That the Better n' Ben's wasn't better than anything. That water could freeze in the kitchen sink a mere fifteen feet from the source of our heat. That our fantasy of cozy nights by the fire wasn't going to come true this winter either.

We also discovered a few things about passive solar. Most importantly, that it really does work.

On sunny days, even with freezing temperatures outside, the living room, with its thirty feet of glass, warmed up comfortably. But there was also a downside to all that glass. As soon as the sun passed into the western sky, or on cloudy days, the glass acted as a heat exchanger, drawing the warmth out of the house to such a degree you could actually feel cold currents moving through the room like a chilly breeze. Sometimes, I'd actually look around to see if Art had opened a window or door.

We also spent a lot of time wishing we had an air lock, a kind of entry room between the outside and the living space. Our west side entry door opened right into the house, letting huge amounts of cold air in and heat out every time we used it.

The Better n' Ben's was a stove meant to warm up a room, at best. And because we didn't have the thousand plus dollars a new stove was going to cost, we'd lulled ourselves into believing Ben was going to warm up 2500 square feet. Packed with wood and glowing red, it was too hot to stand within three feet of, yet beyond that, the heat became ephemeral. Facing the stove, your front side was on fire but your backside was freezing.

When everyone came home for Christmas that winter, I remember hearing Michael and Greg talking one morning. They were sleeping up on the third floor, which had four of those big Cambridge windows and two roof windows, and a lousy wood stove cranking away two floors below.

"Do you believe how cold it was up here last night?" Greg said.

Michael grunted. "Every time I stuck my head outside the blanket, I thought my face was going to fall off."

We passed out four blankets per bed, and there was lots of yelping and hooting every night when it was time to slide between freezing sheets.

Tima Smith

But we needed more than extra blankets on the beds. We needed a bigger stove and we needed to keep whatever heat it supplied *inside* the house.

Our biggest problem was still a lack of cash. And then a major miracle occurred.

For two years in a row, I'd applied for a National Endowment for the Arts Fellowship. Those were the days when the NEA was well-endowed and the government accepted a responsibility to promote the arts and artists.

There were hundreds of entrants, and I knew winning was a long shot, so after I sent my application off, I didn't give it much thought. Then one day the phone rang and Art answered. It was Jerry, friend and fellow-writer. Art listened for a second, then he looked at me, and I could tell that whatever he'd heard had amazed him.

"Jerry says you won."

"Won what?"

"An NEA. He says your name's on the list of winners. He just got it in the mail."

For a minute I was sure Art was kidding. Or Jerry. But a writer would never do that to another writer. I got on the phone and Jerry read my listing. Just my name and state on the Fellowships For Fiction list.

Brian was there that day, too, and once it sank in, once we realized I'd just won a twenty thousand dollar fellowship, he and I grabbed on to each other and jumped around the room for a good two minutes while Art stood there grinning at us.

The day the check arrived, we stared at it a lot longer than made sense.

"I told you, didn't I," Art said. "I always knew you were going to do something like this some day."

"But I didn't believe you," I said. "You're *supposed* to say things like that. It's your job."

He shook his head. He smiled. "Anyone who could straighten out that chimney can do anything."

It had become a theme with us.

I've published many stories since then, even a few novels. But that prize was the first and the best. And it wasn't just the money, although it was an amazing amount and couldn't have come at a better time. It was receiving recognition that really counted. Because like most writers, there were always questions in my mind … was I wasting my time? Was writing a luxury I really couldn't afford? What if it never paid off? What if I really wasn't very good? Yes, writing was one of the most important things in my life, but when it came right down to it, in practical terms, wasn't it a selfish, illogical thing to pursue?

And now this had happened.

We made a to-do list, and the first item read *Warm Up!*

We looked into passive solar window coverings, which mainly consisted of quilted fabric panels attached to frames. The panels slid up to let the sun in during the day and down to keep the heat in at night. They were handsome and convenient and each panel cost triple what we'd paid for the window it was supposed to cover.

There were methods for covering roof windows as well. Polystyrene beads that spilled into a second window below the roof window at night or on cloudy days and then were magically sucked away at a touch of a button when the sun came out. The price was astronomical.

We had some money, yes, but we wanted to make it go as far as possible. Besides, we'd gotten used to doing things our own way.

We went to a local fabric mill and bought two bolts of upholstery fabric, one blue, one gray, and one bolt of cotton batting. I was no Betsy Ross, in fact I'd almost have preferred re-

Tima Smith

digging the utility trench to sewing those curtains, but I was desperate to be warm.

    I cut and pieced the fabric so each window blanket covered either two or four of the living room windows. The blue fabric faced in, the gray faced out, and the batting was the filling. I stitched the edges, folded the top to make a pocket for the metal rods Art was cutting and installing, and then put in three or four rows of grommets, depending on the size of the window blanket, top to bottom. The grommets held the three layers together, so I avoided having to quilt stitch, which I probably couldn't have handled anyway. We threaded thin nylon braided line through the grommets and then through hook eyes high on the wall. At the top of the blanket, each line turned in the same direction, going through each hook eye, becoming one hanging braided cord to raise and lower the entire blanket.

    When down, the blankets covered the entire glass area, except for the grommet holes, which were small enough not to be a problem. When up, the blankets folded into a fairly neat bunch above the windows. They worked perfectly.

    And it was amazing what a difference they made. We'd raise them in the morning, when the backs were warm from the sun, and lower them when the glass felt cold in late afternoon. No more heat being drawn out through the glass. No more drafts.

    I made window blankets for the second and third floor out of comforters. They kept us warm on winter nights for many years. And we installed a ceiling fan on the third floor directly above the stairwell. We keep it going all winter, pushing the heated air down from the ceiling peak.

    We went shopping for wood stoves and discovered that all U.S. wood burning stoves in the late '80s were manufactured, by law, with catalytic converters to keep their emissions down. But catalytic converters begin to degrade from the first fire and eventually interfered with the stove's function. We also discovered that the Canadian government put money into wood burning research, and that Canadian stoves burned cleaner without catalytic converters than U.S. stoves with them.

We bought a Canadian stove, a Regency, their largest model. It had a glass door, a good-looking design, and a two-speed blower to move the hot air into the room. I call it a 'one-match-stove' because once it's cold enough outside to keep it running twenty-four hours a day, you rarely have to ever restart it. If we fill the wood box around eleven at night and damp the stove down, there's enough of a coal bed left in the morning to start a fire simply by throwing in some kindling and logs.

Its capacity is more than adequate as long as the outside temperature is above 20 degrees Fahrenheit. If the temperature dips below twenty and there's no sunshine, the inside temperature averages from around 65 in the living room to as low as 55 in the furthest second floor bedroom. We put on wool socks and an extra sweater. But even on a very cold, sunless day, the third floor is always pretty comfortable — all that heat rising up the stacked stairwells!

If the temperature goes down to zero, which it occasionally does one or two nights a winter in Connecticut, well ... then it's a little tough getting out of bed in the morning. When we know we're headed for single digits, one of us usually sleeps down in the living room and gets up every two hours or so to keep the stove going full-blast all night long.

A few years ago, we installed electric baseboard heat in the bedrooms. But we only use it for company.

Most of the time, we're quite comfortable.

***

The next thing we did to warm up was draw up plans for a mudroom — a good-sized addition on the entry side of the house, big enough to hold a supply of firewood and all the various outdoorsy things we had no storage for yet. That mudroom made such a huge difference in keeping the house warm, we decided that if we enclosed the entire perimeter of the house with one, we wouldn't need any heat at all.

Beside the window blankets, the new stove, and the mudroom, we scoured the inside of the house for air leaks, adding insulation, foam, or caulk wherever we felt air infiltration. It all made a difference. And once winter stopped being something to anticipate with foreboding, we could look back at those first two awful winters almost as something of a lark, an adventure, a test of our endurance.

CHAPTER TWENTY-FIVE

Re-Doing What Should Have Been Done Right The First Time Around

THE SHOWER THAT LEAKED

We finally acknowledged to each other that the shower was leaking about three years after we started using it.

Until then, we'd chosen to ignore it. Maybe we hoped it would fix itself. But when it started dripping right through the ceiling boards into the utility room below, we had to face the fact that we'd done a really bad job water-proofing the shower. In fact, we hadn't water-proofed it at all.

In hindsight, it's hard to believe we could have been so dumb. Dumb enough to lay a concrete floor over wood without a waterproof membrane in-between. But that's what we'd done.

We'd put in a marine plywood base, as though the word 'marine' meant water-proof, which of course it doesn't. And how could we have ignored the fact that cement plus wood plus water equals one very bad combination!

It probably took no more than a couple of weeks for the concrete to become saturated, even though we put four coats of sealer on it. And of course, as it aged, it would have contracted slightly around the edges, creating a groove for water to seep down into.

And I'll admit it right off the bat. The upper parts of the shower, the ceiling and the walls were Art's project. They never leaked a drop. The base, the concrete? Yeah, that was mine.

Tima Smith

It's a very fancy shower. For one thing, it's very large, with plenty of room for elbows and whatever. Art started off by backing the walls with Wonder board, a water-proof cement board specifically for bathroom applications.

Once the Wonder board was up, it was my turn to do the floor: a marine-plywood base covered by about six inches of cement. It turned out swimmingly. The cement had a gentle slope from the walls to the drain, and I polished the surface so it was smooth underfoot. Then I waterproofed it. And, for some crazy reason, I decided *that* was sufficient.

We'd bought packaged cedar tongue and groove boards for the finished walls, and Art went to great trouble to construct those walls with air channels between them and the Wonder board so air could circulate and allow no possibility of trapped moisture and eventual rot.

And when it was done, it was a fabulous-looking shower. The first truly-finished part of the house. We were so anxious to be clean again, to feel hot water on our skin. We installed an overhead light, shelves for shampoo and soap. It was our first symbol of civility — attractive and utilitarian at the same time.

And then the damn thing started leaking like a sieve!

We read up on shower floors. Ah-ha. A shower pan, that's what we'd left out. We'd put one under the washing machine in case *it* overflowed. How had we possibly thought that a concrete shower base, a porous material to begin with, taking a direct soaking many times a week, wouldn't need the exact same thing?

You can't imagine how much we did *not* want to deconstruct that shower. We needed to break out the entire concrete base, probably remove the cedar walls. We'd be without a shower again for days, maybe weeks.

We tossed it back and forth, looking for something else that might work, and came up with an answer. More waterproofing. And caulk, lots and lots of caulk.

Fifty Acres, More or Less

The shower stopped leaking, at least visibly, and we breathed a sigh of relief, figuring we'd managed to avoid tearing something out and redoing it when so many things still remained completely undone.

It took about two more years before we actually began to smell the rot and the ceiling down below began to drip again.

This time, Art rolled up his sleeves and waded in. He took down the cedar boards, carefully, so he could reuse them. Then he took a sledge hammer to the concrete. A gutsy thing to do considering what he found.

I was upstairs at the computer, letting him have plenty of swing room. "Get the Raid," he yelled up to me. "Carpenter ants!"

We'd supplied them with exactly what they loved. A soft, wet, mushy mass of rotting wood.

Once the ants had stopped twitching, we stood there and looked at what used to be a solid three inch floor. Three-quarters of an inch of plywood, three-quarters of an inch of homosote, and one-and-a-half-inches of tongue and groove pine. The plywood was pulp. The tongue and groove pine was eaten through everywhere except around the edges. The in-between layer of homosote was moldy layers of muck. Even the bottoms of half the shower wall studs were gone. The only thing that still had any integrity was the bottommost layer, the three-quarter inch shiplap pine. Not much of a thickness to be holding up all that soaking wet weight.

"I have no idea what was keeping it all up," Art said. "It wouldn't have taken much for one of us to step in and end up riding that piece of concrete straight down into the utility room."

Art cut or simply peeled away the rotten wood, removed the rotten flooring below along with the bottoms of the studs, and replaced it all. Then we ordered a very large piece of vinyl shower liner, with corners and glue and complete instructions.

We installed the liner, poured a thin cement base, reset the drains, and installed a tile floor for the shower. We also tiled about a foot-and-a- half up the walls, as well. I sanded the cedar, treated it with an oil sealer, and Art put it back on the walls. We had our shower back.

And now it doesn't leak.

THE ROOF CAP THAT LEAKED

Another thing we had to redo was the roof ridge cap. We'd been especially aware of the problems a heavily insulated house can encounter, hearing stories about several roofs that rotted in a matter of years because of insufficient air circulation between the insulation and the plywood sheathing. We'd planned the sheathing on the walls carefully, but the ceiling insulation was thicker by several inches, and we wanted to be certain that air vapor wasn't going to turn to moisture someplace within the combination of fiberglass, plywood, and shingles.

We had a continuous air flow between the plywood and the insulation from eave to peak, but we'd chosen an aluminum ridge vent that was supposed to do away with the need for applying a layer of shingles over it.

It allowed for good air circulation, but it leaked whenever there was a particularly hard wind-blown rain. And it wasn't very attractive either. Eventually, Brian took the initiative and replaced it with a tough plastic sponge-like ridge vent that consists more of holes than plastic, covered with a folded layer of shingles. No more leaks. And the roof looks better.

THE PROTECTAION ONLY PAINT SUPPLIES

In order to avoid exterior upkeep, I'd treated the exterior of our used Anderson windows with marine urethane. But after a few years, it was obvious that wasn't enough. After reapplying the urethane once or twice, I realized what a good protection paint really is. So a few years ago, I painted the exterior of all the wooden windows light brown to match the vinyl cladding on the new Andersons. At the same time, we painted the fascia on all the eaves. It gives the house a more finished, unified look, and the oil-based paint is holding up well.

THE STAIRCASES

We ripped out our temporary first-floor staircase and built a new one, pre-figured this time so that each step has the same rise. We built a pantry under those stairs with lots of storage, and then, since we were still using the wall ladder Greg had banged together to get to the third floor, we built a set of stairs directly above the first floor staircase. It felt almost decadent, having those stairs, and for months, whenever I wanted to get to the third floor, I'd walk over to the place where that wall ladder had been. Habits, even uncomfortable ones, are hard things to break.

Tima Smith

CHAPTER TWENTY-SIX

HURRICANE

We never admitted it to each other until much later, but when we heard that Connecticut was in the direct path of Hurricane Bob, we got scared. Were the nails holding the roof rafters together at the peak long enough? Had six at each joining been enough? Were the metal tie-downs we used big enough?

We'd intended to finish the third floor ceiling with pine tongue-and-groove boards, but it was a big expanse and, therefore, a big expense, and we'd kept putting it off. So now, in August of 1991, we were still staring at a ceiling of insulation backing paper, and I couldn't get out of my head the nagging idea that an integrated tongue-and-groove wood ceiling would have added a good degree of integrity to a roof that was going to have to stand up to hurricane-force winds.

We stowed away all loose outdoor items, pooh-poohed at least two suggestions to ride out the hurricane off the hill, filled some containers with water, filled the kerosene lamps, and bought new batteries for the flashlights. Then we hunkered down and waited.

Art ended up spending the hurricane on the third floor. I think he wanted to be there in case something bad started to happen, so he could see it early and order an evacuation. I stayed on the first floor, pacing, while I listened to the roar of the wind, and to the house groaning with every heavy gust. I watched the trees bend double and wanted it all over quickly.

Although hundred-plus mile per hour winds were clocked near the shore, our winds probably never exceeded seventy-five, but they were strong enough to strew the yard with a mass of broken tree limbs, branches and leaves, and drop a tree across the driveway. The house came through fine.

As it turned out, it wasn't the hurricane that would live in our memories as much as its aftermath. *That* was the real disaster. We were without electricity for over a week, which meant no water, no flushing, no refrigeration. Plus, there was one more thing that arrived during the aftermath of the hurricane. The last thing either one of us expected.

Benjamin, Art's old friend, the tactless one who'd never got over his doubts about Art and the 'tangent' he'd been on for several years now. He'd been absent for two or three years. But the day after the hurricane blew out, Benjamin called (somehow, the phone was still working) to say he was blowing in. He was on his way to a nearby conference and could he stay with us for a night?

"He wants to stay *here*?" I said to Art. "Does he know we just had a hurricane? Did you tell him we have no water, no electricity? Did you tell him it's not your typical house yet?"

Art nodded. "He said it doesn't matter. All he needs is a bed."

Of course I knew there'd have to be more to it than that. Food, for instance. And social niceties ... which, I remembered, had been a bit strained the last time he visited.

But Ben was far from a top priority as we began clearing the debris from the yard and driveway, threw out all the food decomposing in the fridge, carried pails of water up from that old well that had kept us in shower water when we first began building. Each day, we assumed the electricity would come back on. But it didn't. And then we heard that it would be a week or more until our area, always the last on the block, was restored.

Art tried to call Ben, but Ben was on the road and unreachable.

"He'll stop at a motel when he hears how bad things are here," Art said.

But three days after the hurricane hit, Ben came walking up the hill.

"I tried *four* times to drive up your driveway," he said, "when the hell are you going to pave that thing?"

"Well hello," I said, "nice to see you, too."

He hadn't changed a bit.

We explained that thanks to Bob we were without electricity and water, but that we had plenty of bottled water, and Art had driven a ways and come home with a 24-hour supply of food that didn't need to be refrigerated or cooked.

"Fine," Ben said, reaching into the doughnut box and coming up with a chocolate frosted. He poured himself a glass of water. "Got ice?"

Truly, I did my best to be empathetic. I knew that Ben had lived in Brooklyn most of his life, a city boy through and through. He worked in academe. He'd never camped out or peed in the woods. I was pretty sure that to him, a group of ten trees was as good as the forest primeval.

Actually, though, he seemed a little impressed by the house. "It's so…" he waved his hand above his head, "…high," he said. "You knew how to put a roof on?"

"We learned," Art said.

Ben nodded. "Well … if it didn't blow off in the hurricane, I guess that's a good sign, huh?"

He admired the view. He thought there should be more white walls. "Too much wood," he said, "all those knots." He liked the high ceilings. He didn't like the open stairs to the third floor, which we'd built without risers. "You could slip right through," he said.

"Well," Art said, "maybe if you were the size of a small cat."

It took him a good five minutes to figure out that when we said we heated with wood, we meant we heated the *house* by burning *wood*. In that square black thing over there called a wood burning stove.

"But what if it goes out?" he said. "What if you go away for two weeks in February? You have a furnace in the basement, right? That makes heat all by itself?"

"We stick around in the winter," we said. "Because we can't let it go out. If it did, our pipes would freeze and … well, you get the idea. And no, we don't have a furnace. We don't even have a basement."

Ben shook his head.

It took him a while to make the connection between our water and our well pump and our lack of electricity, so he kept trying to flush the toilet. Then it occurred to him about ten p.m. that he wasn't going to be able to take a shower in the morning. I told him we'd set several pails of washing water in the shower.

"Oh," he said, "so I just pour it over me, right?"

"Well yeah," Art said. "But remember, it's cold."

"Cold?" Ben said. "Can't we heat it up on the stove?"

"No electricity," Art said.

"Oh right," Ben said. Then his face lit up. "How about the wood stove? Just make a fire!"

I looked at Art to see if he wanted to make that particular sacrifice, but he didn't seem to. "It's August," he said. "It's 92 degrees in here already." He grinned. "Which will make that cold water feel great."

Ben looked doubtful. "Got an alarm clock I can borrow?"

Art shook his head. "Nothing wind-up," I'm afraid.

"But I have to be in Rhode Island by nine. I have to be sure I wake up by seven."

"I'll knock on your door," I said. "Seven sharp."

"How will you wake up without a clock?"

"I always wake up around six," I told him. "I can tell by the light."

"What light?" he said, as though he thought I might have access to some mystical illumination that said it was time to get out of bed.

"The morning light," I said, gesturing toward the windows. "The sun. It wakes me up."

"Oh," he said. "That."

At bedtime, we gave him a flashlight and showed him to his room. He examined it with his flashlight beam as though he was looking for something specific. Critters? Indications that the ceiling might collapse on him at three a.m.?

The next morning, his eyes were red, his hair was sticking up all over the place, his face was pure scowl, and although I didn't really want to ask, I did anyway. "How did you sleep?"

"Not one wink," he said. "For one thing it was hot. And for another, there were those damn ducks all night. Christ, all they did was quack. I tried closing the windows, but that only made the room unbearable."

"Ducks?" I said. "Ducks?"

"You didn't hear them? There had to be dozens. Maybe a hundred. Right outside the window. They made a racket the whole damn night."

By then, Art had joined us. "What about ducks?" he said.

Ben threw his hands in the air. "They quacked all night. She didn't hear them." He pointed at me. "But I sure did. You must have heard them, Art. Don't tell me you were able to sleep through it? Because nobody could sleep through that night after night."

Art looked at me. "Ducks? We have ducks?"

I shook my head. "No ducks. No water. It was tree frogs."

A million tree frogs sang me to sleep every night from August until the first hard frost. And I suppose if you weren't used to it, it *was* a racket.

"What the hell are tree frogs?" Ben said.

Fifty Acres, More or Less

I put up my hand and held my thumb and forefinger a few inches apart. "Tiny little frogs. Arboreal. They sing at night."

"You call that singing?" Ben said.

I shrugged. "We're used to it. Just like you probably don't hear the sirens in Brooklyn."

He looked at me as though I had to be defective to see any correlation between the two things.

Later, Art told me Ben took three doughnuts with him, declined an offer of a ride down the hill to his car, and patted Art on the shoulder when he left. A gesture of sympathy.

It was the last time we ever saw Ben.

That night in bed, we lay there listening to the tree frogs. Ben was right, it *was* loud. One of my favorite sounds on the hill.

"Boy," Art said, "those are some damn noisy ducks."

Tima Smith

CHAPTER TWENTY-SEVEN

WAS IT WORTH IT ALL?

We continued to finish the house little by little over a very long time. We learned patience.

Every year we do something to make it more comfortable. And after years of disorganization, we've added a lot of fixed storage — cubbies for mail, drawers for tools, easy access to kitchen paraphernalia. It all provides a particular sense of satisfaction.

I could point out something in almost every room that still needs finishing. But now it's something we elect to do, rather than a frantic necessity.

The interior of the house is finished almost exclusively with wood — ceilings and walls. Here and there on the second and third floor we used plasterboard, generally where we wanted a quick finish. People who offer opinions site plasterboard as a good option because it's so inexpensive and because it offers relief and contrast from all the wood. "If you'd used plasterboard everywhere," they say, "you'd have been finished a lot sooner and spent a lot less money." Point taken. But Art and I prefer the wood. Plasterboard is heavy and awkward to handle, easily damaged, and labor intensive in its own way. Plus we've discovered there's an art to plastering the seams, one neither one of us ever acquired.

Most of our walls are finished with either the free pine we got from Bill Lambot or six and eight-inch wide tongue and groove pine. Most of the ceilings are done in eight and ten-inch shiplap pine. For smaller ceiling areas, like the second floor bathroom and hallway, we went with 'bead-board' or 'porch ceiling,' narrow, beaded spruce you often find on porch ceilings and the wainscoted dining rooms of Victorian houses.

All the ceiling wood had to be stained and given two coats of urethane before it went up, a time-consuming, tedious job. But once it's up, you never have to touch it again. We used Minwax stain, either Golden Oak or Puritan Pine, light stains that bring out the grain but don't darken the interior by absorbing light.

There have been long stretches of time when we've turned our attention to the outside … clearing trees to widen a view, turning brushy woodland into clear areas and gardens.

We still look for bargains on building materials. We waited a year for a specially-ordered but never picked up eight-foot tall Anderson glass door at Home Depot to come down in price from nine to three hundred dollars. We gambled and won on the fact that no one would buy such a tall door, and it became our exterior door onto the deck on the east wall. (A deck we hadn't built yet.)

The first day we spied the door, we offered the store manager three hundred dollars on the spot. He smiled and declined our offer. Two months later, the price was seven hundred, then five, and eventually we gave him what we'd offered a year earlier and he gave us the door.

***

NATURE

Snow, Snow, Snow

The house has survived blizzards and nor'easters. The pine siding has weathered to a deep gray. On sunny winter days, the passive solar keeps us comfortable, and if it's not sunny or if the outside temperature dips below ten degrees, we make sure the wood stove is cranking and we wear long underwear.

We have enough wood on these fifty acres to keep us passably warm for a long long time, although providing that wood is a more or less constant job. We cut trees during the winter for the following year, and try to have the logs cut and split by the end of May. We figure we handle each piece of firewood six or seven times before we finally toss it into the stove.

Tima Smith

Winters are a special challenge, and we had to switch to four or all-wheel-drive vehicles early on. They climb the hill like a goat under all but the worst conditions, and never slip going down, never spin you around in a wild circle or take you for a sideways ride off the edge of the driveway and into the woods. To deal with ice, we scatter the ash from our wood stove. It works far better than sand. In all the years we've been here only two plow trucks have actually made it to the top of the driveway pushing snow all the way. One arrived at the top pouring steam from a burst radiator hose. That was easily fixed. But the other seized its engine and had to be towed the next day. Nobody ever offered to plow us out again.

So even though it seemed impossible, we were forced to figure out how to clear the driveway, at least the steep part, by ourselves. An old plow truck we bought made it down once, but never made it back up again. A regular-sized snow blower Greg brought here one day was hopelessly inadequate.

The solution we ended up with was pretty basic. A shovel.

I have to admit that the first time I started off with it to clear one tire path eight hundred feet down felt completely insane. But it wasn't the shovel that failed. It was our stamina that needed building.

I take one tire track, Art takes the other. In three hours, we have wheel and walking tracks and the sun does the rest. I'll admit it's not something you look forward to, shoveling half of a 2000 foot driveway (we have someone plow the flat part), but at night, when there's not a sound in the world except the squeak of your boots … when the snow is reflecting the moonlight … when you're warm despite the fact that it's seventeen degrees … then, shoveling a thousand feet of driveway isn't anywhere near as awful as it sounds. And if an owl happens to land in a small tree about five feet away and sits there watching you for a few minutes before flying silently off into the night, well, that's something you don't easily forget.

Still, the weatherman has special power here. We listen carefully. A prediction of anything over a foot and a half of snow, puts us on high alert. Snow maroons us, locks us 2000 feet away from roads and stores and mobility. Occasionally, if what's coming sounds particularly bad, we might park the car down near the beginning of the driveway. But getting to that car and then getting back to the house can be something akin to an heroic trek.

If there's sufficient snow, the grandchildren we now have will tell you that sledding down the driveway is the most scream-inducing ride you can get.

Lightning

We've discovered that lightning seeks out well pumps, with two hit so far at a thousand dollars each. Which proves that nothing, even your own well water, comes free. And it occurs to us during thunderstorms that we live in a tall house on a high hill. Lightning has hit as close to the house as fifty feet. It littered the yard with the chunks of the top half of a sixty-foot larch, blew out two computer modems, turned the air bright inside the house, and generally scared us to death. We've thought about installing a lightning arrestor, but haven't yet.

Ticks

Lyme ticks require constant vigilance. I've had Lyme Disease twice and Art has had erlichiosis, a potentially much more dangerous tick-borne disease, twice. But with antibiotics, we've had no lasting effects, and considering how much time we spend outside, especially around places where ticks are known to abound (stone walls and brushy areas), we've managed pretty well.

Family

Our family has grown.

Lauren is married and has two sons and a daughter. Despite those rough first years here, she chose to have her wedding pictures taken with our view in the background.

Greg is married and has three children. All his practice in Connecticut paid off when he rehabbed a turn-of-the-century farmhouse in Massachusetts a few years ago and then put on a big addition.

Brian lives on the west coast, has two daughters and a son, and occasionally uses the skills he picked up here even though his career is in computers.

Michael is a videographer and often manages to get stuck helping us split next winter's firewood.

Jennifer is a family therapist in Connecticut. Her present skills probably would have come in handy way back then.

Michael E moved to the west coast a few years ago. He says part of the fun of visits is looking for the new things we've done since he was here last.

***

So, Was It Worth It?

In a word, yes. To justify everything we went through while we created this home, I suppose one has to believe that the place where one lives is vital to one's existence not just as protection from the elements and a holder for stuff, but as an integral part of one's consciousness.

I've lived under roofs all my life, but I've never felt particularly nurtured by any of them. Now I feel nurtured.

Looking out the window in the winter, I see hundreds of bare branches, glimpses of green, an expanse of sky, formations of geese, a lone hawk, the tops of distant hills. For me, there's a decided effect from the breadth and scope of the exterior of my living space on the breadth and scope of my psyche, and winter is precisely the time I need to see far, to contemplate imagined potentials, to examine possibilities.

In the spring and summer, nature closes in, blocks off the views both in and out, encloses us for several months, but that's when we actually experience it most directly. There's grass to cut, gardens to weed, the encroachment of vines and wild roses to keep back, road upkeep, house work, walks. It's not a time for reflection, but for involvement, a time when the moment becomes the focus, and, at least for a while, we can pretend that winter will never come again.

Fall, quite simply, is magnificent.

***

When I think about those first few years, working so hard to get a roof over our heads, I see it as both crazy and brave. For certain, I know we'll never again do anything that requires so much hard work and so much sheer determination. It was a once-in-a-lifetime experience.

There are moments we still talk about, laugh about, groan about…

the first night we spent here, before we'd put a shovel into the ground or made any decisions about what was going where. We'd borrowed a small tent, and as the night descended, these woods became a very different place, empty of all the sounds I was used to … traffic, planes, cars … but filled with noise … peepers, rustlings both large and small, owls, dogs — or was it actually a coyote howling in the distance? A sudden nearby screeching in the woods turned out to be raccoons fighting or mating — a noise that froze me inside my sleeping bag and made me wonder if I was cut out for this sort of thing after all. That night, I could never have imagined myself walking down the dark path between the house site and the cabin without even a flashlight, as though it was nothing more than a familiar hallway. And today, the noises outside, the noises the house sometimes makes, it's all come to fit like a glove. Home.

Tima Smith

the skeleton of the house with the reflection from the setting sun turning the white stud walls red. They were evidence of one of the most basic and earliest human urges, to provide oneself with the safety and security of a living space. Yet, it was so far removed in complexity and expectation.

the chipmunks. We'd been cutting trees and clearing the front yard of brush in an effort to get more sun through the south-facing windows, when we found a nest of four tiny chipmunks, their eyes still closed. It made us feel awful to think we'd destroyed their nest, and where was the mother? We left them as long as we dared, hoping the mother would return, but when she didn't, we brought them inside. I phoned around trying to find out how to care for them, and, ironically, one vet said simply that I couldn't, that it was illegal to interfere with wildlife. "Then you're saying I should let them die?" I asked. She didn't seem to have an answer. The Audubon Society had a more practical approach and gave me the information I needed. I started feeding them with an eyedropper every three hours around the clock, and after a couple of days, they opened their eyes. They grew. And then one day, as if their wildness came upon them in an instant, they were suddenly impossible to handle. I brought them outside and released them, and all that summer I could tell which were my chipmunks and which were not. If I saw one running along the stone wall and spoke, my chipmunks would hesitate, turn and look at me. The others would simply vanish into a crevice between the rocks.

the first meal I cooked in our kitchen. It was spaghetti, nothing special. But to have a stove, to be able to boil water, to sit down at a table and eat something hot, *that* was amazing.

the boy who came out of the woods. It was late afternoon, getting dark, and he was wild-eyed, panicky. He told Art he'd been lost for hours, that he and his father had just moved into a house about three miles away and he'd decided to take a walk. Art drove him home to a frantic father who was just about to call the police. We already knew how easy it was to get turned around in the woods because it had happened to us. But we had our dogs with us and simply gave up thinking we knew which way to go and followed them. They took us straight home.

dropping a tree on the car. Of course, that was me. "Think you should move it?" Art asked, looking at the car. "I don't think the tree's tall enough to go that far," I said. And with my last cut, the top branches went straight through the windshield.

taking the door off a pickup. That was me, too. I was only backing up a few feet, so I left the driver's door open, forgetting about the tree beside the path.

the owls. It was an icy cold winter night, but the sound of an owl close to the house pulled us to the door. We could see one owl silhouetted against a starry sky on the branch of an oak tree about thirty feet away. And there was another calling in the distance, but somewhere far off behind us. We stood there shivering, listening as the second owl drew closer and closer. Finally, something huge swooped low and silent just above our heads and joined the first owl in the oak tree. "Did you see that?" we both whispered at the same time.

the coyote. Coyotes, along with fishers and wild turkeys, were reintroduced into Connecticut sometime in the mid '90s, and turkeys have become a familiar sight now, especially every winter under the bird feeders where we spread corn for them. We've never seen a fisher and don't expect to, but we often hear the coyotes at night. One day I was driving down the driveway when something loped across the road. I stopped. Was that a dog? It started to climb over a stone wall, but hesitated with its front paws on the wall and turned to look back at me. It was bigger than I would have imagined. With a beautiful gray and black coat; intelligent, appraising eyes. It was in no hurry, and we looked at each other for a good fifteen seconds before it finally turned and went on its way.

Tima Smith

the dirt hill that wasn't dirt. Art and I often take walks along the old railroad bed, most often about a mile down to a farm. One sunny winter day, with no snow on the ground, we decided to walk farther and to cut through the field opposite the farm. There was a huge hill of dirt at the entrance to the field, and Art went around it, but I chose to go over it. I took about three steps up the side before I sank in right up to my knees and a ripe, exquisite smell enveloped me. The thing I'd stepped into was a great big hill of cow manure, all warm and smushy just under its frozen surface. And it was like being stuck in quicksand. Art had to pull me out, and he might have done it faster if he hadn't been laughing so hard.

the first new houseplant I bought. Which, for me, turned our house into a home.

Fifty Acres, More or Less

XIII

 These interim chapters could have ended after the white Cadillac left Florida. Because what happened after that really doesn't have any bearing at all on my life. But when you start a story, is it fair to leave off the ending? Probably not. So I won't do that.

 Twelve years went by. Not one of my children heard from their father. Not all of them were at peace with that, but their lives moved forward and other things pushed his absence aside. And then one day, my mother, who had lived in the same house since the 1930s, received a letter from my ex, which she forwarded to me. In the letter, he wrote that he was in AA, at Step 8 (where you need to make amends to those you've hurt) and he wanted to get in touch with his children. I sat with that letter for a few days because, frankly, it filled me with dread. If I didn't share it with them, all of whom were adults and probably deserved to make up their own minds about how to respond, was I doing them a favor? And if I did share it with them, and the sharing resulted in what I expected, was I doing them a disservice?

 I finally decided to tell them. Because he was their father and they deserved to know he was alive and wanted to see them. Each one's response to the news was swift, emotional, and difficult. It made me realize that it's the absent parent who can come to represent the possible, whereas the present parent can only offer what's real. I gave them his phone number. All but one called him, and that son simply said that nothing his father could say or do could ever make a difference.

 Four of them went together to see him. Their father brought a girlfriend, which put a damper on the meeting, exactly, I believe, what he meant it to do. He acted as though nothing particularly momentous had ever happened. He talked about tennis. About what he did for a living. Nothing was said about his leaving, his not getting in touch, about his missing them. He never said the word 'sorry.' They were supposed to meet again for dinner that evening, but only two of them went. The two that chose not to go never saw him again after that. Of the two who did go, one had an on-again, off-again phone relationship with him that petered out after a year or so. The other started a relationship with his father, one that lasted for several years, and involved a compassionate effort to help his father in many different ways. But that finally ended, too.

I don't know what to discover from everything that happened before those twelve years or after. There's no way to make sense of it, to find logic in it, to even make peace with it. Except that you live with things the way they are, because you have no choice. Accepting life is accepting the chaos that's so much a part of it.

The only thing to add, perhaps, is his version of the boat story, which differed little from the one I already knew, but contained a few more details. And perhaps more drama. But then, it was a dramatic tale. One where all reason and rule were thrown to the winds and everything proceeded according to the necessity of the moment. Where he did what he needed to do in order to avoid calamity, even though what he was doing was nothing less than the definition of calamity.

According to him, the idea started one night in a bar. He told some people he had a boat, a big boat, one he intended to sail around the world. But now his ex-wife had it locked up and was preventing him from following his dream. He told them he knew how to get the boat out, launch it, and wouldn't that serve her right, wasn't that exactly what she deserved? Except, he said, he couldn't do it by himself; he needed help. And by the time the bar closed, he had a crew.

He researched the papers that would convince the authorities he had rightful access, then forged them. He and his crew broke into the boat builder's. Then he went to the police and requested their assistance getting the boat to the wharf. He paid well for their help. They accepted his ownership papers, asked few questions. The boat was successfully launched. It attracted attention. It was a big boat that stopped traffic and created a bit of a parade. And when the boat hit the water, everyone cheered. They waved as he and his crew motored off into deep water. Bon voyage.

He barely made it into international waters before he was stopped by the Canadian Coast Guard. They were suspicious of his papers. They wanted him back at port. But then the American Coast Guard arrived, claiming they had jurisdiction because the boat was in international waters and the ownership papers were issued by the U.S. Eventually, the Canadians gave up, but the American Coast Guard wasn't sanguine about the situation either. They put a decal on the boat, marking it as 'unregistered' but, for some reason, didn't put it under tow. Everyone agreed that the boat would put in at the first U.S. dock until things were cleared up. And then the coast guard left. The crew removed the decal and took off.

There were chronic problems with the undersized motor, which constantly overheated because it was only meant as a back-up, not as the boat's sole method of locomotion. The sails were in Massachusetts, paid for and ready to be picked up, but he was afraid to put in, thinking I would be there with the police, waiting to confiscate the boat. So they decided to skip the sails and just kept motoring, slowly making it down the inter-coastal waterway with that malfunctioning motor alone. Once in Florida, with no sails, little equipment, and probably little money, he insured the boat, then took it out into deep water and opened the petcocks. According to him, he was drunk or high or both, and lost control of the rubber raft putting it in the water. He was far from land, the big boat was sinking, the raft was gone. He assumed he was going to die. But after half an hour, he was still treading water and decided to at least make an effort and swim for it. He made it to the beach.

I think he lives in a world where he makes it to the beach every day. Where anything that was fine and good in his life is far in the past.

I, on the other hand, feel very lucky to live in a present where every day is the day I want it to be. Where simple things satisfy me. Where I'm rich in family, laughter, love, wonderful memories, and

Tima Smith

where my surroundings nurture me through every season.

Fifty Acres, More or Less

EPILOGUE -- 2003

This is not something I ever anticipated writing. The house project was more or less finished when I wrote what I thought was the last sentence of this book. Our life on the hill had gone on more or less unchanged for twenty years.

But then in April of 2003, Art had a stroke. He was in the kitchen; I was sitting at the dining room table; it was about dinner time, but I'd had something to eat just a few hours before. I was aware of him opening and closing the refrigerator door, walking toward the stove, registering it all out of the corner of my eye.

"Want some of this?" he asked, holding up a plastic container of leftover tortellini.

"No," I said, shaking my head, "I'm not hungry."

It was so meaningless for a final conversation.

I heard a noise, looked up. He was hanging onto the edge of the sink and I knew something terrible had happened. I knew that instantly. It took much longer for me to realize it would never fix itself.

Two months later, I brought him home, after two ERs, two ICUs, four hospital rooms, two acute care rehabilitation facilities, two pneumonias, several infections, and a great deal of mutual distress. The stroke had left him unable to move his right leg or right arm. He couldn't swallow, couldn't speak. His eyesight had been compromised in ways we couldn't really determine. He could no longer read or write, two things that had made up ninety percent of his life.

The doctors didn't want me to bring him home. They wouldn't say he was dying, but they admitted he'd never get any better. They didn't think I could take care of him, but I'd watched the nurses, and I'd also watched Art. He wasn't dying just from his physical injuries, he was suffering mentally and emotionally and I decided that he wasn't going to die in a sterile gray room sealed off from the touch of a breeze and the feel of sunshine. If he was going to die, he was going to do it at home.

After I brought him home, he actually got a little better. Strong enough to sit in a wheelchair for short periods so I could bring him outdoors. Well enough to go for short car rides and see that the world was still spinning along. Wakeful enough to watch all four hours of Sergio Leone's *Once Upon A Time In The West* and laugh silently at *The Return of The Pink Panther*.

Sitting in the wheelchair in the front yard, he'd look up at the sky and the trees and at the view he'd cleared as if he were seeing them all again for the first time. He'd study the house from roof to foundation as though remembering every step we went through building it, a look in his eye as though he was amazed at his own accomplishment, and sometimes with a wistfulness that said he would give anything to have even a little bit of that time back again.

Once in a while, he managed to eat a tiny bit of ice cream, savoring it as if it were a sheer miracle.

And we talked. Or at least I talked and Art listened. He responded with nods, an occasional word, but mainly with his eyes. He said a great deal with his eyes. And there was a silent dialogue, too ... a dialogue of looks and touches, the kind two people develop who have spent a great deal of time together, who have hit some pretty deep valleys together but always managed to climb back up.

Art died on July 30, 2003, early in the morning, with my Michael and me at his side. He'd spent time with his Michael, with Greg and Brian and Jen and Lauren; with our grandchildren — Kelli-Ann, Hayden, Sierra, Carly, and Zachery; with his friend, Jerry.

He was himself to the end — deft, strong, stoic, elegant, gentle, brave. And I miss him every day — that wry, witty humor, his ironic, canny sense of the world, his sharp brilliance and quiet

humanism. But at the same time, he is around me in every fiber of this house we built together. And that is a great comfort.

EPILOGUE -- 2016

It doesn't seem possible Art's been gone for a dozen years. A dozen! The first two without him were very bleak. But then life slowly kicked in again. More grandchildren arrived, for a grand total of nine. And there's always so much to do! Firewood needs cutting, fiction needs to be written, money needs to be earned, dogs needs to be walked. And that damn driveway needs to be kept up.

So I do it. And more.

A deck. I'd been staring at the empty space along the east wall for a very long time. That's where the deck was supposed to be, and the porch. But the only thing there were two doors opening onto nothing. I'd stand and stare at the space, alternately thinking I could never build a deck all by myself and wondering who would do it if I didn't. That went on for years. I'd decide it was an impossibility and simply start thinking about something else.

But on a day in early May 2013, for whatever reason, *not* doing it suddenly felt worse than trying and failing. So I roughed out a pattern of more-or-less evenly spaced cement posts on a piece of paper, got my shovel, and started digging.

I'd gone through the same kind of inner conversation so many times by then. *Why on earth are you doing this? It's crazy! You've lived just fine without a deck for thirty-five years. Why now?* And like every other time, I gave myself the same answer: *Just shut up and dig.*

Tima Smith

I dug one 36" deep hole. Sure, it wasn't the most fun I'd ever had, but it wasn't all that hard, either. Besides, a hole could always be filled in if I felt out-matched, right?

Twenty-one holes later, I bought twenty-one tube forms and set up level strings across the thirty-foot by sixteen-foot area. Once I had an idea how tall each pier had to be on the sloping ground, I started bringing home bags of concrete. I couldn't pick one up and carry it, but I could slide each one off the tailgate of the truck into a wheelbarrow, push it to the other side of the house, mix and dump, mix and dump, mix and dump.

I inserted re-bar into the wet cement in each form for strength and although it took a month, I eventually had the base of the deck. Twenty-two concrete piers. And now, with those immovable piers all sticking up out of the ground, I was in the place I needed to be — too deep in to back out.

I built the base using lumber I could handle and laminating it until it was of sufficient size to hold a strong deck. I needed help moving the longest support stringer, a thirty-foot long beam consisting of three sections of three 2x10s nailed together. But by then I had Hayden, a very strong seventeen-year-old grandson, who brought along a friend to help and then went off on their trail bikes through the woods.

After the base was in place, the decking was easy. Light cedar boards that smelled like heaven.

My three dogs had a place to laze in the sun, while I fastened the cedar with a hundred screws. The deck was done by the end of August, and it was beautiful.

My head suddenly sprouted all the other big projects that needed doing.

Windows. All those huge marvelous practically-free windows from that Cambridge building had been gradually failing, getting cloudier and cloudier every year. After all, they were second-hand when we bought them in 1986. Plus, there was new energy-efficient glass that would let the sun's heat in and not let it out again. And those old window blankets I had stitched so many years ago were way past the end of their lifespan.

So I ordered eleven windows for the first floor and two for the second. Expensive, but not as expensive as I'd anticipated. Of course I couldn't handle those heavy windows alone, but my daughter Jen and her husband Al volunteered to help. The glass company wouldn't deliver the windows. The driveway was too rough and they wouldn't guarantee that all the glass would survive. So Jen and I picked them up very early one morning. It took two trips and we wrapped each window in a blanket and set them on a base of foam rubber. They made it up the hill just fine.

By the end of the day, all the new windows were installed, and all the old windows were in a pile in the back yard. I spent a few days caulking and filling every space where cold air could penetrate. We'd left a lot of them thirty-five years ago. But we'd been in a hurry back then. Now, there was no hurry. I just wanted to do a good job.

And what an amazing difference those new windows made! Sparkling clear glass. No more ancient window blankets, even at night. The proof of how superior the new windows were? I remembered resting my forehead against the old windows on a freezing day and getting an instant headache from the intensely cold glass. But these new windows are never cold. Even when it's below zero outside, which it is far more often now than I remember during past winters – proof that global warming is indeed responsible for more extreme fluctuations.

After that, I spent a summer refurbishing all those elegant old Andersons in the second-floor bedrooms. I took them all out, stripped them, replaced all the glazing, then painted them a lovely shade of pumpkin. Thirty-five years has darkened the siding to a deep deep gray and I decided a bright accent color was needed. They still look great.

Tima Smith

Finally, after two decades, a third-floor ceiling, with just a slight problem. I finally finished the third-floor ceiling with tongue-and-groove pine. It was the first big project I did completely by myself, and the thing that made it possible was the finish nailing gun Art had bought just before his stroke. It was during that job that I probably came closer to disaster than I ever have.

Picture me at the top of a sixteen-foot aluminum stepladder. I'm working above the stairwell, not my favorite place to be. The ladder is standing on two 2x16s that span the length of the third-floor stairwell. It's a little bouncy, going up the ladder, but I know it's sturdier than it looks and feels. Again, however, it's not my favorite place to be.

My next ceiling boards have to go around the ceiling fan, and I have to remove the decorative cap from the fan in order to put the boards in place around the fan's circular electric box. I've turned off the electricity to the fan, but I've spent at least ten minutes trying to figure out that cap. Because the two screws that hold it in place look wrong. They aren't the tiny screws one would expect to hold in place a cap that doesn't weigh more than an ounce. They're hefty. And that doesn't make sense. I go back down the ladder and find the instructions that came with the fan, but they don't help. So I climb the ladder and start to loosen those screws, each a little at a time, and when they come out, the entire fan comes away from the electric box with them.

So there I stood, ten feet off the floor, holding a twelve-pound fan in one hand, my screwdriver and the two screws in the other. And all I can think was ... *now what the hell am I supposed to do?*

I suppose I could have let go of the fan and hoped the thin wiring would hold it up. But it was a *fan*, not a light bulb. Heavy. And if the wiring didn't hold it, it was going to come crashing down on me. Which made it highly likely that I might fall off the ladder. Which, remember, was over a stairwell. Essentially over thin air.

I couldn't make myself take that risk. Somehow, I had to get those screws screwed in again and secure that fan. Except I couldn't see the position of the tiny holes the screws needed to go into because the cap, of course, was in the way.

The fan was getting heavier by the second, and, somehow, I had to hold the fan with one hand, and, with the other, insert a screw without letting it fall out, and then screw it in to an invisible screw hole.

I eyeballed the cap, centered it the best I could against the electric box I couldn't see, jammed one of the screws into the hole, and while I held it in with the tip of one finger, inched the screwdriver against it with the other four.

It took several seconds of finessing, but somehow I didn't drop the screw or the screwdriver, and suddenly, the screw grabbed. I tightened it enough to take the weight of the fan, then I fiddled the second screw in, climbed down, and stood there for a minute while I waited for my arms to stop shaking.

It ended up being a less than perfect job of fitting the boards around the fan cap, but it's pretty high up, so I don't think anyone will notice. Unless they read this.

A porch. I loved the deck, but what I'd really always wanted was a screened porch. So about two years after I built the deck, I decided to do the porch. I didn't tell anyone. I was so tired of all that eye-rolling. My kids had gotten used to me doing things I know they thought I shouldn't. They'd stopped protesting. But I could *hear* their thoughts.

I always wished Art were here every time I started something new, because he was the design-man, and I especially wished he were here to design that porch. I had no idea if I could pull it off. Would it end up a mess? A parallelogram instead of a rectangle? And how was I supposed to figure out where I could attach the structure to the house? How did I know where the studs were inside the wall? And now I was going to have to drill holes again. What if I missed a stud and hit and electric wire? What if I hit a knot and the drill spun and broke my wrist? I thought about all these things day and night. And gradually, I worked it all out. Or at least I was pretty sure I had. And what if I *did* break my wrist? Well, it might slow me down, but it would heal.

    Thing is, I hadn't planned for the porch when I was building the deck. I knew that the upright beams for the future porch needed to sit on top of the cement piers that held up the deck, but that's where I discovered a slight problem. One of the cement piers below the deck was situated smack in the middle of the patio door. (That was just a hard thing to admit.) How had I *done* that? But for some reason, I'd done something else ... I'd extended the deck several feet beyond the back wall of the house. I think I'd had some vague idea that I wanted a porch door in that five-foot extension. A lovely pumpkin-colored door that would be approached by a stone path along the back of the house. Hmmm.

    Because of that extension, I was able to shift the porch enough so I didn't need that unavailable support pier. It had nothing to do with skill. It was just plain luck.

    And if you're *really* lucky, you have a son named Greg who takes pity on you when you get to the 16-foot roof beams that you can't even pick up, never mind carry up a ladder and set in place, and who will come and help you get them where they need to go, and then help you finish the roof. In that case, you're really *really* lucky.

***

    So now the house is pretty much the way we envisioned it over thirty years ago. Oh, there are *still* things to finish ... a third floor bathroom, not a hard thing to do, but certainly not a necessity. Closet doors are still missing. And I need a new roof. But that's not something I'll be a part of.

    And, oh yes, I also have a brand new, big idea. (Those were announcements Art always met with a certain look.) This idea includes ripping up that awful still uneven brick living room floor, putting in piping for radiant heat, and replacing the floor with something nice and smooth and even ... cement? Maybe. Or better yet, tile! Then solar on the new roof to power the radiant heat, and voila! I would have to produce a lot less firewood every year.

Well ... we'll see how things work out.

Odd, how I think I miss Art more, rather than less as the years go by. He nodded okay when I asked him to come back for me when it was time. And I suppose that time is drawing closer. We'll have a lot to catch up on. I have so many things to tell him. How that tiny granddaughter named KK who he used to push endlessly on the swing has grown into a wonderful young woman who works in an ER and heads off to PA school next year. And that little boy who used to build things for hours in our living room with leftover ends of 2x4s and Papa's hammer? Well, Hayden's going to be an engineer some day. Remember the little girl who used to sing *This Old Man* over and over from the back seat? Carly's a track and field star now, and she has the biggest brown eyes in the family. Sierra, who still lives in CA, may be on the east coast next year for college. She has a great eye for style and design and wants to have a career in visual communications. Maybe we'll watch her on TV some day.

And then I'll have to tell him all about Zach, who's already fourteen and makes fantastic videos and knew everything about WWII by the time he was ten. And Trevor, who's passionate about baseball and has a knack for anything mechanical; and Emerson, who shares Trevor's passion for baseball and looks just like Brian; and Allison, ice skater, ballerina, and the fastest learner I've ever seen; and then the youngest, Alexa, who quite simply sparkles. And I'll tell him that thanks to them and their parents, the last decade has been good to me. Full. And wrapped with new memories.

Then, I'll be sure to tell him that my time with him ... every single minute of it ... was, quite simply, the best time of all.

BOOKS BY THIS AUTHOR

SHORT STORY COLLECTIONS

AFTERNOON DELIGHT BOOK I

AFTERNOON DELIGHT BOOK II

AFTERNOON DELIGHT BOOK III

AFTERNOON DELIGHT BOOK IV

AFTERNOON DELIGHT BOOK V

COW HORMONES

NOVELS

CLICK

DON'T LOOK DOWN

A DANCE WITH THE DEVIL

PAYBACK

LOVE CANAL

RIDDLE

STINKBUG

50 ACRES MORE OR LESS

MOON OF THE DARK RED CALVES